AF255664

CONTEMPLATING COUNTRY

FAITH AND JUSTICE IN THESE LANDS NOW CALLED AUSTRALIA

This series explores issues of faith and justice in these lands now called Australia. Each book in the series examines a particular topic of injustice in Australia and asks how Christian faith and discipleship shape a just response. Authors come from many Christian traditions, ethnicities, and theological backgrounds. These authors reflect on contemporary issues through the lens of Christian faith and biblical justice. Authors explore such topics as Aboriginal and Torres Strait Islander experiences and contributions, homelessness, women's rights and women in leadership, family and domestic violence, mission and discipleship, bullying and harassment, multiculturalism and ethnic diversity, sex and gender issues, refugees and asylum seekers, disability rights, climate change and environmental protection, security and terrorism, unemployment and job security, political polarization, church decline and health, faith in a secular age, leadership scandals and church abuse, and more.

The vision of the series is for faith and justice in these lands now called Australia—justice first for the land and the sovereign people who belong to this country and then for other marginalized and vulnerable groups. Jesus calls his disciples to love mercy, seek justice, and walk humbly with their God. This series explores that call and shows how God's people are responding with courage and conviction.

EDITORIAL TEAM

Editor in Chief
Grahem Joseph Hill

EDITORIAL BOARD

Darrell Jackson
Darren Cronshaw
Garry Worete Deverell
Gina A. Zurlo
Grace Ji-Sun Kim
Graham Joseph Hill

CONTEMPLATING COUNTRY

More Gondwana Theology

"From the Depths, Life Rises" by Glenn Loughrey

GARRY WORETE DEVERELL

foreword by ANNE PATTEL-GRAY

WIPF & STOCK · Eugene, Oregon

CONTEMPLATING COUNTRY
More Gondwana Theology
Faith and Justice in These Lands Now Called Australia

Wipf & Stock
An Imprint of Wipf and Stock Publishers
199 W. 8th Ave., Suite 3
Eugene, OR 97401

www.wipfandstock.com

PAPERBACK ISBN: 978-1-6667-8844-0
HARDCOVER ISBN: 978-1-6667-8845-7
EBOOK ISBN: 978-1-6667-8846-4

VERSION NUMBER 10/03/23

Contents

Foreword

I was humbled by Garry's invitation to write the preface for this book as this is an honor he has bestowed upon me. As two of only a small handful of Aboriginal theologians in this country, it is a privilege to acknowledge Garry's contribution to theological scholarship. In *Contemplating Country: More Gondwana Theology* Garry shares a certain vulnerability with his readers as he exposes the pain of our people but also our capacity to thrive through an intentional cultural and spiritual connection to country.

Garry has a gift for articulating what many Aboriginal Christians feel and know deep in our bodies, precious pearls which—whilst fragile and permanently at risk in the dominant culture—we yet long to share and bring to expression. His articulation of our Christ, for example: the one who is country and in culture, the one who is the source of our strength and our flourishing. For non-Indigenous Christians this book may at times be challenging and perhaps confronting, but it is worth the read as it names a destination that few have journeyed towards, and that is the Aboriginal soul at the heart of this country. This book provides an account of Indigenous epistemologies, cosmologies, and theologies that will help the reader navigate our unique cultural protocols, our understanding and management of country, and even our approach to church.

There is a great need for the non-Indigenous Christians of Australia to hear the voice of First Nations theologians and church leaders. Indeed, there is a challenge here, in Garry's book, to not only hear the voices but also to genuinely listen to what is being said. I don't know why our voices aren't being heard or what it will take for the churches to hear the voice of Christ's people who are oppressed and suffering under continued colonial subjugation. Is it really because we have no worth or value? Are hearts so hard and cold that our cries for justice simply cannot penetrate? Or is it because our voices call the churches to account for their role in the theft of our land, and cultural genocide, and the destruction of our environment?

There is so much we Christians in Australia must address if we are to be "reconciled." There is an assumption, for example, that the Australian churches once had a positive relationship with us that has somehow been fractured. But this isn't the case. The only relationship that is documented in our history is that of Indigenous people as the objects of white missionary endeavors to suppress our way of life and forcibly Westernize us, leading to our dehumanization and subjugation. The churches have a lot to atone for, particularly: their participation in the theft of our land, our economic base, thus leaving us in multigenerational poverty; and their kidnapping of multiple generations of our children, breaking families apart and destroying communities, a sin which still unfolds today as church agencies remain willing agents of government policy. The list of sins is a very long one and some are highlighted and discussed in this book. How do we speak of reconciliation when historically there has never been a healthy relationship between white and black Australians, especially not one of respect for Aboriginal people or value for what we bring to the table?

Garry's book opens for the reader an Aboriginal perspective which reframes and decolonizes received theological understandings of the Trinity, Christ, Scripture and—through his exegesis of country—the ecological crisis that confronts all Australians. Garry's explanation of why we acknowledge country is exemplary, and his discussion of the parlous state of reconciliation in the churches is simply prophetic. This book will be of great benefit to all Australians of good will and open heart, all who believe that redemption may have something to do with receiving and living a more ancient truth.

Professor Anne Pattel-Gray
School of Indigenous Studies
University of Divinity

Series Preface

Faith and Justice in Australia

This series explores issues of faith and justice in the settler colony of Australia. Each book in the series examines a particular form of injustice and asks how Christian faith and discipleship might contribute towards a more just response. Doing so necessarily requires that Christians first take a good hard look at ourselves, describing and acknowledging our own racist attitudes and practices. Racism in this colony has flourished since the very first contact between invaders and native Aboriginal and Torres Strait Islander peoples. Within the realm of the churches, racism manifests itself in the benign and unproblematic way we understand our history, as well as in contemporary ecclesial cultures, theological paradigms, educational curricula, and governance structures. More insidiously, racism remains a constitutive part of what might be called the "colonizing" imagination of whiteness.

Each book in this series is peer reviewed under the oversight of an editorial board. The peer-review process ensures quality research and writing, aids in vetting and selecting books for publication, and provides suggestions for improving the books accepted in the series. This process enhances the quality of the books published in this series.

The series considers a wide range of injustices, inequalities, and oppressions in contemporary Australia. The editors invite and welcome contributions from many Christian traditions and theological perspectives. Authors will reflect on contemporary issues by creating a fruitful dialogue between Christian tradition (in its broadest sense) and the lived experience of minority communities. Such communities may include First Peoples, women in leadership, the homeless, those exposed to family and domestic violence or workplace bullying and harassment, migrant communities, refugees and asylum seekers, LGBTIQ+ communities, the differently abled, and the environmental matrix which native peoples call "country." Authors may tackle issues around environmental protection, security and terrorism, unemployment and job security, political polarization, church decline and health, faith in a secular age, leadership scandals and church abuse, and more. Some authors will utilize the tools of deconstruction and decolonization; others will draw from the liberative traditions of class, gender, ethnic, and environmental studies. Whatever the case, all authors in the series will seek to engage critically with culture, Bible, and theology, and acknowledge that every churchly activity in the colony occurs on lands and seas that were stolen from Aboriginal and Torres Strait Islander peoples.

That is to say that, in the opinion of the series editors, we cannot consider the multiple injustices at play in Australia without first taking account of the primary and original sin of colonization. "Australia" is, in fact, an ongoing colonial project which builds racism, injustice, and ecocide into the very fabric of things. It began, here, with the invasion of the British from 1788 onwards, and continued with the stealing and destruction of land and waterways, peoples, cultures, and livelihoods. Today Indigenous communities continue to be plagued with deaths in custody, massive over-representation in the justice system, soaring suicide rates, and consistently poor progress on indicators around health, wealth, and education. Sacred sites continue to be destroyed without consequence, local ecologies continue to degrade, and species continue to be threatened with extinction because corporations and governments control and mismanage native land. The colonial project remains pervasive, and Christians have made significant and ongoing contributions to its success.

It is the view of the series editors that the first issue to be confronted by any proposed series on an Australian theology of justice is the problematic nature of "Australia" as a colonial project. If this is not done, then every issue addressed will repeat the ontological and epistemological practices of dispossession and displacement, which are the true font and source of most Australian theological performance. Only theologians who have acknowledged and addressed the colonial project will be able to generate the tools they need to respond adequately to the many subsequent injustices that plague our nation.

The authors in this series won't just focus on injustice. They will also examine a biblical theology of justice and highlight ways Christ's people are already working toward justice, peacemaking, healing, and reconciliation in the colony. The biblical witness affirms that God cares deeply about justice and calls his people to act justly and work towards a just society. "The Lord has shown us what is good. And what does the Lord require of you? To act justly and to love mercy and to walk humbly with your God" (Mic 6:8). The God of Isaiah exhorts the people to "Learn to do right; seek justice. Defend the oppressed. Take up the cause of the fatherless; plead the case of the widow" (Isa 1:17). The God of Zechariah commands that we "Administer true justice; show mercy and compassion to one another. Do not oppress the widow or the fatherless, the foreigner or the poor. Do not plot evil against each other" (Zech 7:9–10). The God of Proverbs gives us no other option but to "Speak up for those who cannot speak for themselves, for the rights of all who are destitute. Speak up and judge fairly; defend the rights of the poor and needy" (Prov 31:8–9). And the God called upon by the Psalmist commands us to "Defend the weak and the fatherless; uphold the cause of the poor and oppressed" (Ps 82:3). Church communities that follow these commands and take them to heart will be genuinely prophetic: they will provide a radical alternative to the colonial business as usual. They will be communities filled with transformed nonconformists (Rom 12:2).

The Bible repeatedly urges us to embrace God's heart for justice and mercy. There are more than two thousand verses in the Bible on poverty and justice. Our world is crying out for justice. Jesus calls us to be a prophetic church committed to justice and compassion. Scot McKnight, a New Testament scholar and author, comments on how often the Law and Prophets combine God's will (*mishpat*, etc.) with righteousness and justice (*tsedeq*, *tsedaqah*) and how wide-ranging that *tsedeq* is. Deuteronomy 16:19–20 says, "Do not pervert justice or show partiality . . . Follow justice and justice alone, so that you may live and possess the land the Lord your God is giving you." Amos 5:24 uses *mishpat* and *tsedeq* in parallel and could be read as "Let 'judgment' and 'justice' roll down like waters, and 'right conduct' and 'righteousness' like an ever-flowing stream." Doing justice involves both good judgment and right conduct in acting with and on behalf of the disadvantaged in societies. Furthermore, the righteous will and judgment of God is the source of our concern for justice. Time and again, the Law and the Prophets say that God's will is that his people be a people of righteous conduct and compassionate justice.

Having said that, it is important to acknowledge that the Bible is not entirely consistent in its representation of the divine voice. It is a text which, historically, has been used to justify genocide, ecocide, slavery, patriarchy, and heteronormativity. The view of the series editors is that the Bible freezes in time multiple theological perspectives at times of political or theological crisis for its readers, and that these perspectives do not always agree with each other. Some biblical texts are frankly abhorrent to the modern reader, especially those of us who have learned what justice might mean from texts found in the same Bible. What this means, theologically, is that human persons are responsible for our interpretations. We cannot say, consistently, that "God says" without saying, at the same time, that "we *discern* God to say," thus foregrounding the possibility that we are as fallible as the biblical authors themselves. The authors in our series will therefore be as critically aware in their treatment of the biblical witness as they are with Australian church and society.

Governments, businesses, and humanitarian organizations have an essential role to play in addressing poverty and injustice. But the church must never lose sight of its own vocation. Governments and other secular organisation cannot deliver redemption or restorative justice in all its fullness; restorative justice also includes the activities and actions of moral and theological communities such as the church. In many Christian circles, mission and evangelism are out, while social justice is popular. But true justice always combines social concern and activism with gospel proclamation, biblical faithfulness, evangelism, and mission, and healthy church life. The local church is paramount in God's mission. Humans need justice and liberation, but they also need personal redemption. This is not a matter of *either-or*. We are *first* the church of Jesus Christ, witnessing to Jesus's redemption, gospel, and justice through our life together and in the world. We are *then* the church that serves among and influences governments and other organizations. This is not a matter of *either*-or but one of *first-then*.

In Luke 4:18–19, Jesus echoes the words of Isaiah 61, including the proclamation of good news for the poor and the Lord's love for justice. The Lord "upholds the cause of the oppressed, gives food to the hungry, sets prisoners free, gives sight to the blind, lifts up those who are bowed down, watches over the foreigner, sustains the fatherless and the widow, and loves the righteous" (Ps 146:5–9). The Messiah, who is God's chosen servant, "proclaims justice to the nations," caring for the bruised and broken (Matt 12:15–21). Jesus condemns religious leaders and institutions that neglect justice, mercy, and faithfulness (Matt 23:23). Jesus makes it clear: ". . . whatever you did for one of the least of these brothers and sisters of mine, you did it for me" (Matt 25:40). Jesus challenges his people to respond to injustice and show God's peace, justice, and reconciliation—this is at the heart of discipleship and the gospel. The prophetic church sees this and responds. God calls us to proclaim and usher in a new age of justice, equality, healing, and freedom.

The volumes in this series don't merely focus on injustices in Australia and necessary responses by those of the Christian faith. Authors also explore how God's people are already seeking to be voices for justice in this nation—speaking up for the poor, protesting the treatment of asylum seekers and refugees, feeding the hungry, housing the homeless, protecting vulnerable women and children, loving neighbors, welcoming and advocating for religious and ethnic minorities, providing affordable food and healthcare, engaging in political and policy advocacy, building communities, and more. The vision of the series is for *faith and justice in Australia*—justice first for the land and the sovereign people who belong to this country and then for other marginalized and vulnerable groups. Jesus calls his disciples to love mercy, seek justice, and walk humbly with their God. This series explores that call and shows how God's people are responding with courage and conviction.

Graham Joseph Hill
Garry Worete Deverell

Dedication and Acknowledgments

The theme for this year's NAIDOC celebrations is "For our Elders." I therefore dedicate this book to my parents, John and Elaine, with thanksgiving for all you taught us about country and about Christ.

Several of the pieces that appear in this book began life as occasional posts to my blog, which can be found at https://uncommonprayers. blogspot.com.

I want to thank those who read this text prior to publication and whose input greatly improved its content, especially Auntie Anne Pattel-Gray, Meredith Lake, Lil Deverell, Naomi Wolfe, and Uncle Glenn Loughrey. The remaining errors and faults are, of course, mine.

Uncle Glenn has again provided the art that graces the cover of this book, and again it communicates far more than my words could ever pretend to do. Thank you, Uncle, for all your support and help.

Some of the more significant material in this book arose from discussions with my students in the School of the Indigenous Studies units on theology and Bible. I thank you all for your willingness to participate so energetically in those conversations.

Finally, I thank the general editor of this "Faith and Justice in Australia" series, Graham Hill, along with Greta Morris, our copyeditor, for all their skill and helpfulness in getting this manuscript from computer to press.

Introduction

Aboriginal and Torres Strait Islander peoples are incurably obsessed with the land, sea, and skyscape we call "country." We have a relationship with country which is usually more respectful than that of colonists. Where romantically inclined immigrants look for the serenity of "untouched nature" or long for the solitude and peace of "wilderness," Indigenous people look to country for the teaching of our creator ancestors in the lifeways of plants, animals, and precipitation. Where miners, foresters, and pastoralists seek to squeeze profit from country, Indigenous people ask how land, sea, and animate creatures might serve and care for each other. Where religious folk, particularly from the city, might look to country as a place of "retreat" from busy lives, a place where human stress can be managed and wonder reignited, Indigenous people seek to fashion and cure country in ways that will relieve the stress our environment is under and apply certain medicines to her grievous wounds.

This is a book that seeks to explore the meaning of country *theologically*. It assumes that whatever the damage done by colonists to country and to Aboriginal and Torres Strait Islander culture and livelihood, there yet remains something that is good and of lasting value in the "gospel" they brought with them over the seas. Some will wonder at this. Some will argue that the colonial imagination is so violent in its impulse towards obliteration and possession that there can be no good news for Indigenous peoples even in the "good news." These same critics will say that there is little difference between a resources company which knowingly destroys sacred sites and churches who effectively clear-fell Indigenous knowledges in favor of what they see as an infinitely better way. Such critics, because they cannot imagine a way in which colonists and colonized might engage in healthy and mutually beneficial conversation, will likely read this book as yet another example of the dispossession of Indigenous people of what is rightly ours.

Still, this is a book that seeks to explore the meaning of *country* theologically. It assumes that country is a sacred text, that country is wise and can teach human beings to be wise in ways that even the Christian gospel is only dimly aware of. That I take the wisdom of country seriously will, of course, be deeply troubling for some, especially Christians of the *sola scriptura* or *sola ecclesia* varieties. Those who believe that we can learn nothing of the purpose of our existence outside of Bible or church will find here some deep challenges. For, as a member of that community which has enjoyed a living relationship with these lands since the beginning of creation, I cannot abandon the accumulated wisdom of that experience simply because some recently arrived whitefella tells me to. Whilst, for evil and for good, I have learned a great deal from Bible-and-church theology, this has never been enough for me on its own. For me, as for many Indigenous people, Bible and church theologies only become helpful insofar as they can be incorporated—brought into analogical relationship with—the wider, longer, and deeper traditions which govern our native lifeways in this ancient country. Inevitably, if my critics do not feel that they can learn from Indigenous wisdom, then this book will be regarded as just the latest example of pagan heresy and superstition.

Here's the thing, though. I love the church and I love the Bible. I also love country. I love them all. I am in a vowed or religious relationship with each of them. I am bound to each of them in ways that could not be undone even if I sought, by some heroic act of the imagination, to do so. For each dwells, irrevocably, in both my history and my body. Each has inhabited and become part of me, such that the boundaries between Bible, church, country, and my personal self, are impossible to delineate. That is why, in my theological writing, I try to bring each of these loves into relationship with each other. That is why I seek some kind of effective and useful conciliation between them. I cannot give any of them up.

There is a sense in which this book might therefore be understood as an invitation to a campfire singalong between country, church, and Bible. Church and Bible know each other well. They have been singing with each other for years. Just not here. Not around a campfire hosted by this country. Indeed, when Bible and church more latterly came to this country, they pretended that they were back where they came from. They were so caught up in their own song, the song they brought from elsewhere, that they were unable to hear the local song. Indeed, when some of the visitors finally caught wind of this country's cadences, others acted to repress and drown them out. Country, meanwhile, represents a primordial choir, a polyphonic song that has been happening since the beginning of creation. The song of country is a weaving together of unique and wonderful voices from rocks and waterways, from plants and animals, and even from people. It would be wonderful if Bible and church, the Bible and church that have come from elsewhere, could respect the primacy of our song for this place, for this country. It would be wonderful if, instead of seeking to destroy or transform our song, the visitors could sit with us around the campfire and listen a while. Perhaps the visitors might eventually learn our song, and appreciate it for what it is, in its own integrity, rather than for what it can do to embellish the song of the visitors. Perhaps Bible and church might even learn to sing with us and add their voices in ways that harmonize with country. Perhaps they might then, finally, cease to be merely visitors. Maybe then, they will really belong.

Belonging is possible. Bible and church *can* make their homes in this country as they have made their homes in my own trawloolway history and body. But only by renouncing all fictitious thinking concerning ontological or epistemological supremacy; only by seeing themselves as visitors and not hosts; only by becoming curious, again, about the ways of the divine; only by learning, in a renewed and refigured way, how to love.

This book continues to explore these possibilities by picking up from where my 2018 volume *Gondwana Theology: A Trawloolway Man Reflects upon Christian Faith* (Reservoir, Victoria: Morning Star, 2018) left off. Since then, there have been multiple opportunities to reflect further on our colonial imaginations, churches, and Bible; and upon decolonized versions of Christ, the Trinity, and theological method, upon the ancestral spirit of country, and on many other weighty matters. The essays here represent my attempts, within a variety of settings and conversations, to give voice to the ever-new, ever-dynamic voice of the divine in these lands. I've avoided an appeal to the more familiar forms of settler theology as much as possible. Because a genuinely Aboriginal theology is still so novel in colonial Australia, new containers for theological thought have been invented, probably quite poorly. I pray that there may be many more Indigenous theologians to come who can correct and improve my plodding and imprecise work. I thank everyone who invited or cajoled me into writing these thoughts down on paper and ask that my readers may see them as provocations to yet more thinking and conversation as we continue to wrestle with our complicated Australian history and legacy.

CHAPTER 1

The Rise of an Indigenous Theological Imaginary

NEW DIRECTIONS FOR THEOLOGY IN THE SETTLER COLONY OF AUSTRALIA[1]

Towards the end of 2021 the University of Divinity launched its School of Indigenous Studies. The purpose of the school is to encourage the development of Christian theologies that have their roots as much in Aboriginal and Torres Strait Islander imaginations as they do in the perspectives brought from Europe by settler colonists. Recognizing that most Australian theological activity has been generated by settlers, the school will deliberately seek to both decolonize Christian traditions and to engage them anew, beginning with a uniquely Indigenous sense of relationship with land, waterway, and sky. Through the school, the university's students, graduates, teachers, and researchers (whether Indigenous or not) will be encouraged to form a relationship with Christ that grows from the imaginative roots of the world's oldest living cultures.[2]

This vision gestated over many years through conversations between local and international Christian leaders, both Indigenous and settler. It was often noted that Australian theological colleges and seminaries were run *by* settlers, *for* settlers, and that their curricula invariably reflected this fact. More recently, of course, there has been a welcome influx of new

---

1. This section is an updated version of Deverell, "Our Vision."
2. See University of Divinity, "Vision."

migrants into Australian theological schools and a subsequent expansion of consciousness about the mission of the church. Some schools have even employed people of color as tenured lecturers. But it remains the case, to this day, that no denominational theological college has ever employed Aboriginal or Torres Strait Islander theologians to teach tertiary-level theology in a sustained and ongoing way. Some of us have been visiting lecturers and tutors. Three or four of us have even held down short contracts. But the overall picture remains bleak for our people. Amidst the diverse cultures of modern Australia, Aboriginal and Torres Strait Islander people are still regarded as the "wrong kind of black" to be occupying senior leadership positions in our churches or theological colleges. And that sends a clear and fundamentally racist message to our mobs: "Stay away; you, along with your spiritualities and theologies, are not welcome."

The School of Indigenous Studies aspires to change that. We have begun to offer tertiary level courses in theology that are taught by Indigenous scholars, from Indigenous perspectives, using Indigenous teaching methods. Although the courses are open to any student that meets the academic entry requirements of an Australian university, we have sought to ensure that this particular learning experience offers a safe space for Indigenous students. Non-Indigenous students must therefore agree to refrain, for example, from badgering Indigenous students with inappropriate questions born from Australia's particular talent for casual racism, whether that be conscious or unconscious. All students agree to treat other students with respect, and to accept the ruling of their Indigenous teachers on what that respect looks like in practice.

"What does it matter," many persist in asking, "if theology is taught by settler colonists? Isn't theology just theology? Don't all potential church leaders, whatever their ethnic profile, need to have a basic understanding of the theological tradition to guide their people through the complexities of modernity?" Whilst I heartily agree that every potential ministry agent needs to have a foundational understanding of theological tradition to navigate the complexities of modern Australian life, I am not at all convinced that teaching a settler colonial version of that tradition is going to do the trick. For "theology" is always and everywhere perspectival. The tradition does not speak with one voice, even if that voice is taken to be exclusively settler or colonial. Theology is forever shaped by the places, people, and cultures in which it is written or performed. That is as true of the foundational theological texts found in the Bible as much as it is for every subsequent iteration. And it is as true for "second order" theology (academic-sounding reflections upon theological art or narrative) as it is for the more primary, symbolic forms such as poetry, oracle, parable, painting, sculpture, architecture, dance, sacrament, or "liturgy" (a term which arguably encompasses all the others).[3] Most recent settler colonial theology recognizes this fact. At the same time most settler colonial theology appears blind to the powerfully unconscious filters at play in its own means of production, filters which seek to reduce and simplify as well as to appropriate and colonize theological formulations that come from other places and peoples.

This seems especially true when it comes to settler colonial engagements with Indigenous people. Here in "Australia" (itself a colonial fiction), white theology has pretended for nigh on 230 years that Indigenous people do not exist. For 230 years the theology of the colonizer has worked hand in glove with the legal fiction of *terra nullius* which asserted, and still asserts in many pockets of the settler church that, upon arrival, this continent was entirely without people or culture, that it was effectively a blank canvas which God had provided for the painting of an entirely white future. In this respect, white theology is, as a matter of historical record, remarkably like the Constitution of the Commonwealth of Australia, which makes no mention at all of Indigenous peoples, either Aboriginal or Torres Strait Islander. White theology, like the Constitution, was habitually written in the service of an entirely white, colonial, people with white, colonial, concerns.

Many modern observers, particularly those who have come to Australia more latterly, may wonder at how theology could be as complicit in the Great Australian Silence[4] about Indigenous people as the disciplines of history and politics, and even more so. But the reasons for this are obvious, are they not? In addition to that more habitual form of white filtering that accompanied, and still accompanies, the expansion of colonial empires, here in Australia theology has been silent because of a secret shame that can barely, even now, speak its own name: the shame of knowing that—against every ethical principle that may be derived from the teaching of Jesus or his apostles—the churches were willing partners and agents in the attempted genocide of an entire people. The colonial churches, and/or prominent members of those churches, both enabled and enacted the massacres,

---

3. I owe these notions of first and second order types of theology to David Tracy. See Tracy, *Blessed Rage.*

4. Henry Reynolds reflects upon this phenomenon at some length in his book. Reynolds, *Why Weren't We Told?*

the removals, the enslavement, the incarcerations, the "reeducation," and the wholesale destruction of Indigenous agriculture, language, kinship systems, cosmologies and spiritualities.[5] The churches did this, but their shame at having done so has rendered them silent, especially insofar as the church speaks through its theological performance. It is far easier to speak of the sins of others than of our own sins. It is easier, to cite a prominent example, to endlessly discuss the German theology that emerged from the Nazi holocaust in Europe, than to engage the reality of Australia's original sin and founding act of violence or, indeed, its contemporary consequences across a myriad of social and spiritual indicators.

It is no coincidence, then, that colonial settler theology in this country has barely begun to engage with Indigenous people. Arguably, it has only begun to do so because we, the Indigenous members of the churches, have begun to cast off the imaginative shackles made for us by our white governors and find our own voice. Doing so is, of course, immensely complicated. For every Indigenous person in the country has been colonized, whether we are personally conscious of the fact or not. The tentacles of colonization extend not only to the stealing of land and the destruction of culture, but also into the hearts and brains of colonized people. The colonial prohibition against talking and speaking and acting "like a native" is, at the same, a constant and unrelenting pressure towards adopting a white view of the world, a white social imaginary. I personally know Aboriginal people who identify themselves as Christians or political conservatives, who whilst insisting they are genuinely Aboriginal, also seem to be completely comfortable with unreconstructed, entirely white, accounts of who and what they are, even to the point of baldly stating that colonization was in fact God's way of punishing Aborigines for our supposed wickedness. I find the persistence of such attitudes amongst mob deeply sad and troubling. Having been removed from country, and country from them, these mob are so impoverished in spirit that they cling to moldy mission bread as though it were the fruit of creation. Not their fault of course. But one can understand, also, the charge of "coconut" being uncharitably applied: black on the outside, but white on the inside. Such is the tragedy of colonization.

Of course, the situation with mob in contemporary Australia is far more complicated than reductionist paradigms of color could ever account

---

5. There are multiple histories which cover this period, but see, for example, Harris, "Hiding the Bodies"; Pattel-Gray, *Great White Flood*; Curthoys and Mitchell, *Taking Liberty*.

for. For many of our most capable, and most radical, spokespeople "look" white on the outside but have decidedly black hearts and brains. The paradox here, which routinely seems to bamboozle even the most intelligent colonizer, is that the strongest contemporary critique of whiteness is today coming from Indigenous people who have studied history or cultural studies at the margins of white educational institutions, those ever-fragile margins where Indigenous, or other scholars of color, have enjoyed a measure of freedom to interrogate who we are in our own terms. Here is a particular instance of modernity's inherent capacity for self-contradiction. By making even the smallest room for the other, even if that room is nothing more than a crack in the concrete that composes an urban footpath, in time that gap can enable a seed to grow, a seed that, in time, will transform itself into a large tree which, ultimately, may displace or even destroy the concrete slab.

The Indigenous academics who tend such seeds are doing two kinds of work, simultaneously. We are seeking, first, to recover and reinterpret what can be known about our traditional, precolonial, way of life. In my own field of theology, this means that I soak up as much as I can about the cosmologies and spiritualities embedded in "dreaming" stories, especially those that may be recovered from my own country. This work is frustratingly difficult, especially in the case of lutruwita/Tasmania, because the sheer ferocity of the war waged on our people in the early 1800s came very close to completely obliterating our knowledge systems. What remains, in the accounts of white colonists such as George Augustus Robinson and in a small number of articles apparently coming from the hands of my ancestors at the Wybalenna concentration camp,[6] must be read with a healthy dose of skepticism. Finding the authentic Indigenous voices woven between the layers of prejudicial memory and commentary is painstaking work. But the usefulness for my people of what can be uncovered is beyond priceless. It helps us to understand how our ancestors lived out their sacred relationship with land, waterway, and sky. It also helps us to understand the ways in which our ancestors sought to share this knowledge with the invader, to *translate* that knowledge so that someone from another culture might begin to understand. There are clear analogies here with the work of historical-critical biblical scholars, who seek to recover and reconstruct more ancient voices and debates within the highly redacted texts we must work with.

The second way in which Indigenous scholars seek to water the seeds of a more just future is by offering a critique of the dominant paradigms, the

6. Finlay, *Good People.*

white colonial ontologies and epistemologies by which truth is recognized and evaluated. This, too, is immensely complicated work. The first place from which such a critique might be offered is our traditional knowledge, the weave of ritual storytelling that is commonly called "the dreaming." But, as we noted above, recovering the tradition from its colonial overlays is quite difficult. Very often the Indigenous researcher must simply rely on their innate capacity to discern a continuing voice, the voice of the ancestors, to find where the truth lies. And you do not develop that innate sense unless you spend considerable time on country watching and waiting and listening to its wisdom, especially as that country is interpreted by its custodial elders.

In my theological work, country certainly comes first when it comes to constructing a model of truth and truth-telling. And that means that my critique of other forms of theology, white colonial forms most prominent amongst them, also begins with country. For it is in country that I first discern the voice and activity of the divine. Country is, if you like, an Indigenous Christ. It teaches us who we are, to whom be belong, and what our responsibility or vocation in the world might be. By listening to this voice, I can offer a critique of the white-male-human centered theology that continues to dominate both the church and the society it helped to form. I can analyse their collective complicity in the destruction of the biosphere and their patriarchal and heteronormative gender prejudice and racism. I can reread the biblical texts so that they work with our people and what we know, rather than against us. I can uncover, under all the violence in Scripture, the voice of a divinity who loves the world and its people, and longs for their flourishing, their freedom, and their peace. I can identify there a divinity who is like our wisest creator ancestors. I can even speculate that, perhaps, the God of Scripture and our creator ancestors are one and the same. Though whether this is finally true or not, I could never say for sure.

Why might the study of Indigenous ways of doing Christian theology be of first importance not only for my people, but also for the overwhelmingly white leaders of Australian churches? For Indigenous people, who remain invisible to much of the white church, the possibility of pursing a sense of Christian vocation via an Indigenous-led pathway says, quite simply "we see you, we love you, we accept and acknowledge your world and your ways." Indigenous-led theological study will help us to raise our people from the pits of despair to which we are routinely relegated by settler colonial programs which say, in effect, "you and your ways are not welcome here unless you change and become like us." When Indigenous students can study with theologians who have trodden the same or similar paths themselves, they find that they are no longer alone and that there is, indeed, a place for them in the academy and church. Which is very good news, I assure the reader—breathtakingly good news!

But that is not all. Studying Indigenous approaches to theology can also be good news for white colonists, the kind of good news that Jesus shared with Zacchaeus in Luke's Gospel (19:1–10). For it is clear now, is it not, that white ways and white knowledge have brought the whole of the world to the brink of ecological disaster and social and political implosion? The churches, with their dominantly white-male-human centered theologies, have contributed a great deal to the making of that world, a world in which even wealthy white men will find themselves the unwitting victims of their own blindness. The only way out of this bind, it seems to me, is to turn. To stop listening to the voice of empire and start listening to the people that empire enslaves. For our ways are not the ways of empire. Our ways are about honoring the earth and making sure that every creature under heaven knows their part in preserving its life. In that all people, even white people, will find their liberation and their joy.

WHAT DISTINGUISHES INDIGENOUS THEOLOGY?[7]

What distinguishes white theology from Indigenous theology? This is not as straightforward a question as it might appear. Take the term "white," for starters. What, or who, is "white"? In common parlance, "white people" (meaning people with pale skin) are routinely distinguished from "black," "brown," "red" or "yellow" people. Of course, it is often said that "white" people invented the categories, but that is not quite true. In fact, the people who invented the categories described themselves simply as "people," with no qualifying adjective. For they saw themselves as the paradigmatic model, and everyone else as just a little deficient, somehow.[8] Later on, when those of us deemed "deficient" learned to play this game, we started to call the game-makers "white," which was both a clever move and a stupid move, at the same time. It was clever because it brought into focus the hitherto repressed fact that human beings participate equally in the ontological

---

7. This section is an updated version of the "Foreword" I wrote for Reid, *Isn't It Time?*

8. For a comprehensive account of the invention of race, please consult Heng, *Invention of Race.*

quality of humanness whatever subsequent qualifiers one might then apply, whether that be skin color, ethnicity, gender, or whatever. It was also stupid, however, because by playing the game in this way we who were hitherto "deficient" conceded the game. We conceded, that is, that both the game and its most basic rules were legitimate. We found ourselves, therefore, in an ethical double bind: play the game, but by no means play the game.

A similar dynamic is at play in the word "theology." Those who invented the word were apparently residents of Athens in the fourth century before the "common era." It was a term that found its way into Jewish and Christian thinking because of the colonization of multiple regions and peoples, including Galilee and Judea, by the Greek and Roman empires of subsequent centuries. Following the destruction of the temple at Jerusalem in 70 CE, the *franca lingua* of Jewish and then Christian diasporas was Greek for many centuries: more permanently, of course, in the Eastern Roman Empire than in the West. But the Western (or Latin) forms, which came to dominate European Christianity from at least the sixth century CE, remained essentially Greek in character. Theology, as an intellectual discipline, might therefore be understood as a language game that is essentially colonial: an absorption and modification of first-century events and stories from Roman occupied Galilee and Judea into a larger Hellenistic imagination. This leaves all Christians, even the few who remain in Galilee and Palestine to this day, with an unavoidable paradox: that the Jewish, Aramaic-speaking Jesus and his followers can only be encountered in their Greek versions. Which is to say that the only Jesus we have is already a colonized Jesus. He is a "jew-greek" hybrid.[9] He is, as Heidegger would say, onto-theological: colonized by a totalizing imagination.[10]

Thankfully the repressed are never entirely erased, and those rendered "deficient" still have some agency. The crucified and risen Jesus was able to escape his colonial bonds and inspire multiple movements of liberation and release. Here in the country settler colonists call "Australia," Indigenous people are rising up to claim what has been repressed, destroyed or stolen: country, kin, primordial dreamings. In doing so, some of us are claiming Jesus as an ally. For the colonized Jesus, who in the hands of missionaries and colonial gubbas[11] alike, became a whip to keep us down, can also be seen

---

9. Caputo, *Demythologizing Heidegger*, 7.

10. Heidegger, *Identity and Difference*, 55–71. The irony in Heidegger's concern about a totalizing imagination is not lost on me. He was, after all, a Nazi sympathizer.

11. "Gubba" is Aboriginal English for "governor."

as a gift from our creator ancestors, a gift which can be deployed against our captors. In our hands, the Greek Jesus can become Jewish again by first becoming Indigenous. For he is like us, and we are like him. Together we belong to the great company of "deficients" imprinted with his paschal story:

> We are afflicted in every way, but not crushed; perplexed, but not driven to despair; persecuted, but not forsaken; struck down, but not destroyed; always carrying in the body the death of Jesus, so that the life of Jesus may also be made visible in our bodies. (2 Cor 4:8–10)

This tiny example of Indigenous theologizing reveals, I hope, two things. First, that Aboriginal and Torres Strait Islander peoples will never entirely escape the fact that we are a colonized people. I write in an Indo-European language. I am educated in European intellectual traditions. I am as much Irish and British as I am Aboriginal. I am a Christian. But the second thing this theologizing reveals, I hope, is that I have not entirely lost my trawloolway identity and responsibility to country. I am seeking to reread, to reinterpret, to reimagine as much of the colonial inheritance as I can within that more ancient frame: for the sake of my people, and for the sake of our captors. For our colonial overlords are as much the victims of their empire thinking as we are.

CHAPTER 2

Reframing the Doctrine of the Trinity

MOVING BEYOND "POTTED PLANT" APPROACHES TO THEOLOGY[1]

Aboriginal and Torres Strait Islander Christians often refer to mainstream Australian theology as "potted plant" theology,[2] implying that mainstream theologies are like a series of plants that have been grown elsewhere—in the northern hemisphere, usually—and transplanted here in the "pots" that are settler missions, congregations, books, and theological schools. While these theologies would have thrived and been very much at home in the ecosystems from which they originate, they have only survived in this very different place by being kept in their northern hemisphere containers. Few settlers have felt the necessity to take those theologies out of their "pots" and give them a go in the myriad soils and ecosystems of this country. Not without first removing all the local, Indigenous plants, at any rate. Nor has it occurred to them that the oldest living culture of plant husbandry in the world might have some wisdom to share on that subject. That a dialogue with Aboriginal and Torres Strait Islander knowledges is likely to create a more contextually sensitive and less domineering version of Christianity

---

1. The first part of this chapter reworks material I submitted to *Uniting Church Studies* 1/25 (2023) for a special volume reviewing the recent theological work of Aunty Denise Champion.

2. See, for example, Rainbow Spirit Elders, *Rainbow Spirit Theology*, 3.

should be obvious. But it is not. The colonial imagination of the churches is filled with hubris concerning its own self-importance.

In his Epistle to the Romans, St. Paul offers this analogy concerning the relationship between the Hebrew people and Gentile Christians:

> If some of the branches were broken off, and you, a wild olive shoot, were grafted in their place to share the rich root of the olive tree, do not boast over the branches. If you do boast, remember it is not you who support the root, but the root that supports you. (Romans 11:17–18)

It is a botanical analogy, in which the root of the olive tree is the Hebrew people and the grafted branches are Gentile Christians. The apostle uses this image to argue that the Gentiles to whom he is writing have no grounds for considering themselves superior to Jews. For Gentile faith grows from Hebrew faith and can only continue to live and thrive insofar as it remains grafted to its Hebrew roots. The paradox here, of course, is that St. Paul radically reinterpreted the Jewish inheritance of faith within the new container of Christianity. The primacy of faith in the Torah, law, is displaced by faith in Jesus. Jesus the Galilean teacher becomes Lord, messianic Savior, even God. Whilst St. Paul calls for the Hebrew inheritance to be respected, his own mode of doing so is to change its meaning radically so that it can account for the new experience with Jesus. One might legitimately ask, then, which of the traditions determines the continuing meaning of the other? Is it the Hebrew root that determines the meaning of faith for Christians, or is it the grafted experience with Jesus that determines the "real" meaning of Hebrew faith? On the evidence of St. Paul's letters, I would conclude that it is the latter. The graft uses the root for its own purposes.

I want to adapt this apostolic metaphor for our own context here in the colony of Australia as a way of unpacking the complex relationship between colonial Christianity and Indigenous Christianity. My contention is that Aboriginal and Torres Strait Islander theologians engage with colonial forms of Christianity in a variety of ways, and that these ways might be rendered according to a spectrum or typology of analogical relations between two different plants.

A SIMPLE TYPOLOGY OF INDIGENOUS THEOLOGIES

Aboriginal and Torres Street Islander people are, as you would expect, diverse in our beliefs, spiritual practices, and experiences with coloniality. Some of us were given a choice about whether, or how, we received the colonial gospel. Most of us did not, because Christianity was part and parcel of the control colonial authorities sought to exert over our country, our bodies, and our imaginations. In addition, the churches who were given effective carriage of the settler gospel into our communities did so in a variety of different ways. Some were less draconian and more respectful than others. Most were brutally disrespectful. This messy history issues, today, in four broad types of Indigenous Christian theology.

1. *One colonial plant. Eradicate and replace Indigenous plants.*

    This type of Indigenous theology emerged in communities where the missionaries successfully clear-felled the local plants and replaced them with imported ones. The view, here, was that the local plants were evil and Indigenous "souls" could only be saved by suppressing local culture and spirituality entirely. Once the ground was cleared and the plants poisoned, missionaries could then introduce their own beliefs and spiritual practices from the only seed bank in town. This approach survives into the present day in the Aboriginal Evangelical Fellowship (AEF).[3] Tragically, in my view, such theology is entirely consistent with the dominant forms of conservative white theology in the colony.

2. *Two plants entwined. An Indigenous stump with colonial grafts.*

    This kind of stump and graft theology is explicitly inspired by the relationship between Hebrew religion and Gentile Christian faith in St. Paul's olive tree analogy. Here, Aboriginal and Torres Strait Islander theologians retain the stump of Indigenous belief and spirituality but graft the colonial gospel onto it in such a way that the traditional knowledge is reinterpreted or reframed within colonial categories. Indigenous spirituality becomes a kind of "Old Testament" to which colonial Christianity is the "New Testament." The more ancient spiritual forms are absorbed into the cultural-linguistic framework of the

---

3. See AEF, "Welcome." Note that the AEF's statement of faith, its *credo*, makes no reference whatsoever to Indigenous cosmologies, traditional knowledge, or spiritual practices.

newer, colonial religion which is seen as a fulfillment of the former. Creator ancestors become a "Creator Spirit," for example, and the speaking land of country can only be heard insofar as its teaching is consistent with settler readings of the Bible. This approach would accord, broadly, with that of the Preamble to the Constitution of the Uniting Church in Australia and the work of the Rainbow Spirit Elders.[4]

3. *Two entwined plants. A colonial stump with Indigenous grafts.*

This, too, is a form of stump-and-graft theology, but explicitly reversing the Pauline hierarchy. Here the settler-Christian gospel is reframed or reinterpreted in the light of Indigenous knowledges. Somewhat paradoxically, in this example, the historically older cultural-linguistic framework of Aboriginal and Torres Strait Islander people seeks to absorb the newly arrived gospel of colonists. The settler "God" becomes, as we shall see, the dreaming or kinship matrix, and both "Christ"and "Bible" become country. Arguably, this is the kind of theology I was reaching toward in my 2018 book *Gondwana Theology*, though I wasn't fully conscious of the fact at the time, and there are moments in the book when I clearly slip into a more type two framework, particularly when I am talking about Christ.[5] The current book, especially in this chapter and the one that follows, seek to realign that slippage.

4. *Two plants. An Indigenous tree and a colonial tree, growing side by side.*

This kind of theology neither seeks the eradication of any plant nor the integration of one plant into another by way of a graft. Instead, it seeks to imagine a world in which a local plant and colonial plants may live side by side without either of them becoming the strongest or the most important in some kind of hierarchy. In some ways, this is the kind of theology which is practically operant amongst most Aboriginal and Torres Strait Islander people, regardless of our conscious or personal commitments. For each of us must walk in two worlds, whether we want to or not. When I am with my Aboriginal cousins, for example, I invoke the "ancestors" and "country" and the "dreaming"

4. Uniting Church in Australia, "Revised Preamble"; Rainbow Spirit Elders, *Rainbow Spirit Theology.*

5. Deverell, *Gondwana.*

as primary spiritual categories. And this is the case whether those cousins are Christians or not. But when I am with my settler Christian friends I talk about "Christ" and "Scripture" and the "Holy Spirit." There is little other option, because very few settler Christians seem able to step outside of their assumptions about the world and about truth. That is their coloniality. At a pragmatic level, in other words, we Indigenous people assume that there are two cultural-linguistic frameworks which have their own integrity, and which cannot be readily transformed or even translated into the other. In this fourth type, Indigenous spirituality and colonial theology are ideally able to talk with each other, and even to influence each other by virtue of the communicative genius of analogy and metaphor, but never to the point where they morph into an entirely unified, somehow hybrid, religious tradition. In practice, of course, the ideal is rarely activated because the colonial trees are more numerous and self-absorbed than our own trees, and they generally pretend we don't exist.

One recent example of a theological work that seeks to navigate this more challenging territory is Aunty Denise Champion's book *Anaditj*,[6] which plays with a number of possible positions across the typology I've proposed without ever getting to the point of an explicit resolution in one way or another. Still, if I had to make a call, I would suggest that *Anaditj*, more often than not, gravitates toward a type two theology.

On the one hand, Aunt wants to make a clear distinction between what she calls "the Western faith tradition of Christianity" and her "Adnyamathanha understanding of Anaditj, the way things are." Anaditj, her ancient Aboriginal cultural-linguistic framework, is entirely capable of explaining and making sense of the world. Anaditj possesses its own "deep theological" concepts (p. 7) about the relationship between human beings and country (p. 20). A universal ethic of sharing and reciprocity pertains and is passed on in dreaming stories like that of the Arraru-Mathari cycle. Country, or "Creation" as Aunt often calls it, is compared to the Christian Bible. It is a sacred text in which wisdom can be read (p. 20). She also expresses a dislike for the English word "God" (p. 33), preferring "Arrawatanha," an Adnyamathanha creator ancestor (p. 34).

On the other hand, Aunty Denise has clearly absorbed a great deal of colonial Christianity and made it her own. She renames the multiple

6. Champion, *Anaditj*. In the assessment of the text that follows, I will place page references in the body of my text.

creator ancestors of Aboriginal dreamings "the Creator," or "God" (pp. 12–13) in spite of her stated preference for "Arrawatanha." Aboriginal dreaming stories are themselves renamed as "the much older story" of a "universal Christ" and a "universal church" (p. 13). Here, it would seem, Aunt absorbs Aboriginal stories and spiritualities into the newer language of the colonial gospel. She speaks of the contemporary Australian church being "incomplete" until it takes Indigenous knowledge seriously (p. 15), yet that same church is clearly the fulfillment of everything that was intimated in the long history of Aboriginal knowledge. It is a bigger story that contains the very important, but nevertheless smaller, story of Aboriginal wisdom.

It is clear, however, that Aunty Denise does not feel compelled to do Christianity in the way that most settler Christians would expect her to. She reads the Christian Scriptures, for example, in her own way (p. 8), a way that supports her contention that Aboriginal knowledge is both older than colonial Christian knowledge and has its own, continuing, legitimacy and sovereignty (p. 10). But she is a Christian, nonetheless, and accepts the authority of the Christian Scriptures even as she applies her own kind of interpretation to them and seeks to translate them into her own language.

The mediation Aunty Denise seeks to model between these two religious traditions is around the concept of narrative or story. She notes that "when the missionaries came to the Kimberley to share the Bible with the people, the old people responded that they already knew these stories" (p. 11). For her, religion of any kind can be understood as "Ngalakanha Muda," "Big Wisdom" stories about a Creator (p. 12). Indigenous people have our stories. Christians have their stories. Aunty Denise looks at both and concludes that "God" has been talking to people through both. She recognizes the story that's told in the Bible because "I've heard it somewhere before. It's the echo of a much older story, of the universal Christ and the birth of the universal church" (p. 13). For her, the story of creator ancestors in Adnyamathanha is the same story that is told about God in the Bible. The "God" is the same in either case, they just have different names (p. 40). There was even a "Christ" here, in Aboriginal dreamings, before there was a Christ in Galilee: "Christ was Creator present in our stories" (p. 43). "We don't have to struggle to get people into our churches because Christ is everywhere and in everything and in our story and always has been and always will be!' (p. 46).

Aunty Denise's theology, as expressed here in *Anaditj*, is very similar to that of the revised Preamble to the Uniting Church's constitution, which wants to locate a universal witness to the "Triune God" within Aboriginal and Torres Strait Islander cultures but, by virtue of that very same move, actually displaces traditional Aboriginal renderings of the divine through its preference for the explanatory language of colonial Christian tradition.[7] Here there is a desire to view Aboriginal spirituality and cultural story-telling positively. But what makes it positive is its capacity for translation into settler-biblical categories. This makes both the Preamble and *Anaditj* examples of the stump-and-graft theology of type two, in which the Indigenous—for all its inherent, sovereign, dignity—is ultimately absorbed into the settler Christianity brought to this country by colonists.

I feel that we Aboriginal theologians need to work towards a theology that is more like types three or four, which are less inclined to cede the ground to a settler-colonial imagination, however subtly. I'd rather work towards the recovery of our traditions for their own sake and effectively restart the conversation with colonial religion in ways which take seriously our sovereignty in these lands, and therefore the ontological and epistemological priority of our primordial dreamings for a "Gondwanan" (rather than an "Australian") theology.[8] If that aspiration is allowed to play itself out, then Indigenous theologians will reframe colonial knowledges within local and traditional knowledge systems, rather than the other way around.

What follows is an attempt to do precisely that with the key Christian doctrine of God as Trinity.

AN ABORIGINAL REINTERPRETATION OF THE TRIUNE GOD

Rather than a personal "Father" there is the universal *dreaming* or ancestral narrative:[9] one pattern reproducing itself through differentiation after the model of fractals. Fractals are repeating patterns found in both the biosphere and in many forms of Aboriginal art, whether the "dot" painting of

7. See the more extensive discussion of the Uniting Church Preamble in chapter 11.

8. As noted in my *Gondwana Theology*, this term can stand for a more ancient, pre- or extra-colonial theological weaving.

9. The now commonplace Aboriginal English term "dreaming" comes from the translation work of Baldwin Spencer and Frank Gillen with Arrernte people in the 1890s. It was, and remains, a clumsy translation of *altjirringa*, which is perhaps better rendered as something like "the primordial" or "the great pattern." Still, the translation stuck and found its way into Aboriginal English all over the continent. Today, many Aboriginal groups use it to refer to their most basic cosmological stories and lore concerning the way things are.

the Western Desert or the circular patterns common in Dharug (Broken Bay, NSW) or pennemukeer (Mt. Cameron, Tasmania) country. Whether one is looking at the world at the macrocosmic or the microcosmic level, the same patterns can be found. It is almost as though the DNA of the universe reproduces itself according to a primordial pattern of familial similarity. The point here is that each occurrence of the pattern is unique, singular, an ontological *haecceitas*.[10] Nevertheless, there are obvious family resemblances between each particular dreaming story which come into focus more obviously as a consequence of greater distances between perceiver and perceived.

The point here is not primarily biological or even astronomical. It is ontological and theological. For Indigenous people, the dreaming represents an original and originating set or pattern of all things in which ourselves, our creator ancestors, our country, and all living things, participate. In this context, the word "Father"—if it is to have a continuing legitimacy for Indigenous people—therefore stands for our relatedness as kin, as family, in this universal patterning. It does not stand for a personal being who is literally the progenitor of all creation. It is more about the lore discoverable in country, and the outworking of that lore in ethical relationships of proximal reciprocity with all living kin.

Rather than the incarnation of a personal "Son" we have the cosmic body of the dreaming, which is *country*. Country is the material manifestation of the primordial patterning, by which matter congeals itself into distinguishable animals, plants, waterways, landscapes, people, and heavenly bodies. Country is materiality, creator ancestors who can be seen, heard, touched, tasted, and smelled. Country is the interrelationship of all things in an ecological biosphere; it is the family of plants and animals, but also the collective body of all human beings, Indigenous or settler.

In this perspective there are, in fact, many sons and many daughters of the dreaming. Jesus of Nazareth may be understood as one of them. He may even be understood as one of the more important creator ancestors or "old people." Or, indeed, as a paradigm or parable of the ontological patterning put in play through every form of embodiment or incarnation. In that sense, he is unique, but not uniquely unique. He is one of many, but also a singular embodiment of the patterning of the many. One may note, in this connection, a certain resemblance between the paschal Christ and

---

10. The Latin word *haecceitas* was coined by followers of Duns Scotus to denote the unrepeatable uniqueness of a phenomena.

the capacity of country to reproduce itself through death and rebirth. Or, between the capacity of country to offer itself for the sustenance of all living things and the eucharistic Christ. Or, between the death of country through eco/genocidal colonialism and the crucifixion of Jesus by the Roman State. And so on. The point here is that whatever settler Christians say of Christ, very similar things have been said of country, and for a much longer period in human history. If Jesus is to have a positive and meaningful significance for a decolonized Indigenous theology, he must therefore be understood within that more ancient frame. This simple poem, which I wrote a few years ago for Easter, gives a certain form to these ideas:

> Christ is risen:
>> for and with the little ones,
>> the forgotten and abused ones,
>> the poor and the broken ones.
>
> Christ is risen:
>> into mob,
>> into church,
>> into loving kindness.
>
> Christ is risen:
>> into word and ceremony,
>> into ritual water,
>> into bread and wine.
>
> Christ is risen:
>> into country and river,
>> into air, earth, fire and water,
>> into nova, supernova, and stardust.
>
> Praise him.

Here the *place* of Christ's aliveness, an aliveness reached via death and transformation, is not alongside his personal Father in the otherworldliness of "heaven," but here in this world, this country, this community of being, this cosmos.

Continuing that pattern, let us now consider what might be meant by "the Spirit." Rather than the procession of the "Spirit" from the Father and/or the Son—as in Australian settler theology—there is a procession of the primordial pattern known as dreaming through the incarnations of country and into the material ordering of kinship relations in a matrix of all living things. The Spirit/spirit might therefore be understood as a centrifugal force which makes for relationship: a binding of all bodies together in one body through patterns of reciprocity, kinship, and care; the connective tissue which binds each to each. The Spirit/spirit might also be understood as the voice of country, that capacity of the creator ancestors to communicate with us from stream and mountain and human ceremony, ever reminding and guiding us about where we belong and to whom we are responsible. Finally, the Spirit/spirit might be imagined as the aliveness of country: its animating breath; or the water which flows through its veins; or the fire by which the seeds of new life are germinated. Obviously, these images have much in common with biblical stories about the action of the Holy Spirit. But, again, if the Spirit/spirit is to have a meaningful future in a decolonized Indigenous theology, we must highlight the fact that any such images are drawn largely from the sacred text which is country. Their appearance in biblical texts should therefore be seen as subsequent to this fact, rather than the origin of this fact.

So, there you have it. An extremely brief and compressed reframing of the meaning of the Trinity for a decolonized Indigenous theology, shared more for the provocation of thought and imagination than to paint a total picture. Colonists may dream of comprehensive theologies, but not Aboriginal people, and certainly not me. I see and understand very little. But what I see and understand is important, nevertheless, not least because it is the little things that big, totalizing schemas tend to overlook.

If that rather abstract story is retold in the more concrete form of dreaming story or parable, it might go something like this. The dreaming gave birth to a community of creator ancestors who set about forming the earth, and human beings, and plants and animals and waterways and landscapes, after the pattern of the dreaming. The creator ancestors instructed people, and all the animals, on how to care for each other and for the earth, so that they, and all creation would flourish. Once the creating was done, they rested from their labors by "lying" down in landscape, or waterway, or skyway, so demonstrating their kinship with all they made. From there, the creator ancestors continue to speak to, and guide, sentient beings in their living and caring. There is no distinction in the creator ancestors between an "immanent"community and an "economic" community. You come to know the creator ancestors "in themselves" by observing their activity in the sensible world. There is no distinction in the creator ancestors between the spirit and the material. The "spirits" are always-already manifested in landscape, skyscape, waterscape, and people. They are the binding of these things together in relations characterized by care and love. Let us, therefore, listen to their wisdom.

things together in relations characterized by care and love. Let us, therefore, listen to their wisdom.

CHAPTER 3

Christ as Country

Notes towards an Aboriginal Liturgical Christology

THE VOICE OF COUNTRY

The Uluru Statement from the Heart (2017) says, in part, "We call for the establishment of a First Nations Voice enshrined in the Constitution."[1] While that Voice would take a particular form—most likely an elected group of elders who would offer advice to the federal government on matters affecting Indigenous people—let us not mistake the Voice for simply one voice amongst many voices. The Uluru Statement claims that the Voice would speak from a place of sovereignty which, following the Mabo judgment of the High Court in 1992, is named a "spiritual notion":

> [T]he ancestral tie between the land, or "mother nature," and the Aboriginal and Torres Strait Islander peoples who were born therefrom, remain attached thereto, and must one day return thither to be united with our ancestors. This link is the basis of the ownership of the soil, or better, of sovereignty. It has never been ceded or extinguished.

The voice is therefore, first of all, the voice of what our mobs call "country." Country, for us, is a complex matrix of family or kin: land, waterway, sky, flora, fauna, and human beings. Country is made, in our

1. See "Uluru Statement."

dreaming stories, by powerful creator beings who both shape the landscape and indwell it. As human-animal hybrids, they are the common ancestors of both the human and non-human realms. They are also the connective tissue which makes all life part of one family.

Importantly, this matrix of interrelatedness creates a sense of moral reciprocity between all the parts of the whole. Country cares for us. Country provides everything we need to sustain life for ourselves, our human communities, both now and for countless generations to come. Equally, country needs us. We, as humans, have a responsibility to care for country, to ensure that country is managed sustainably, that we take only what is needful and work hard to live in harmony with the lore that country teaches us through its complex ecological interactions. Traditionally we have learned how to live sustainably as part of country by listening for its wise voice in plant, animal, and season. That is why our dreamings and our ritual storytelling are full to overflowing with the adventures of our feathered, furred, beaked, and scaled cousins.

In Aboriginal and Torres Strait Islander society, if you want to know who you are, to whom you belong, and what you are called to become, you listen to country. And the voice of country is interpreted by elders who have lived within this ecosocial imaginary all their lives and know its voice intimately. We do well to listen to our elders, if we truly want to hear what country is saying. But we should not expect elders to speak with one voice. For the Voice of country is plurivocal. Only by listening to the many and discerning its larger themes will you hear the one across and through the many.

There is, perhaps, a legitimately drawn analogy between "country" and the figure of Wisdom we encounter in the book called *Wisdom* from the Hebrew Scriptures. According to Wisdom 7:25–8:1, wisdom is not simply a creation of the Creator, as it were, from the pure imagination of the divine. Wisdom is an "emanation," the "breath" of the divine. While differentiated from the divine as a feminized figure and form in and of herself, Wisdom is nevertheless *derived* from the divine. "Emanation" suggests that Wisdom participates in the being of the divine creator, sharing the very imprint of the divine DNA. "Breath" suggests that she shares in the animating life or "spirit" of the divine. Here we have the prototype of the emanations or processions of God that Christian theologians (principally from Cappadocia) will later call "Son" and "Spirit" and identify with the Jesus and Holy Spirit of the New Testament writings, principally in the Johannine and Pauline discourses. It is as though Wisdom takes on a body which includes the whole world, the whole biosphere, and animates the whole living cosmos with divine breath or spirit. Amongst the works of Wisdom, by this account, is this:

> . . . in every generation she passes into holy souls
> and makes them friends of God, and prophets;
> for God loves nothing so much as the person who lives with wisdom. (Wis 7:27b–28, Jerusalem Bible)

These three lines tell us three interesting things about the ways in which Wisdom raises her voice in the world.

She raises her voice, first, through generations. Not, that is, just the once, in some especially holy and esteemed moment in history. Some Jews and Christians would like to read the biblical material that way. No. Wisdom, we are told, speaks in every generation. This means that we can legitimately listen for her voice in every time and place.

She raises her voice, second, by entering holy souls who become friends of God, prophets. Prophets, in this Hebrew tradition, are of course those who are chosen by God to be God's voice, the voice of Wisdom. They do not choose this path for themselves. Indeed, they often run away from the very notion because allowing themselves to be so deployed will usually cause both them, and their communities, great trouble and suffering. For the truth Wisdom wishes to speak is often the very opposite of what is either convenient or comforting. We are an acquisitive and self-deceiving bunch, by and large. Indigenous and Hebraic peoples share a great many stories which are designed to dissuade and warn us away from giving into our worst impulses. This is why confession and lament form an important part of both traditions. The prophet, by contrast, is called to come close to the divine in "friendship," to listen to Wisdom's voice, to be remade in the image of divine country and therefore become an agent of transformation for others as the prophet passes on what they hear. By doing so the prophet becomes one who centers their sense of being in the whole cosmic unfolding of divine being, rather than in any sense of single-in-itself individuality.

Centering oneself in personal power, rather than diffuse social and ecological power is, I would argue, the very essence of what the Christian tradition calls sin. Even the most well meaning of liberation movements can be blind to the experience and suffering of others, whether those others be human or non-human kin. Indigenous scholars have critiqued white feminism, for example, for its serial forgetting of black, brown, and

Indigenous women, for its centering of liberation on whiteness and Western middle-class worlds.[2] Such forgetting, far from being merely benign about black, brown, and Indigenous women, actually contributes to the suffering of these women, forming a constitutive part of the death-dealing structures of coloniality.

Finally, then, Wisdom raises her voice by dwelling with prophets. Living with and around and in them so that the prophet can speak from a home bounded by divinity rather than a home bounded, for example, by a picket fence. Or a field. Or a mining company. Or a nation. Or a church. Or a white middle-class feminist collective.

That is not to say that Wisdom lives nowhere in particular, mind. Wisdom in fact lives *everywhere* in particular and therefore prophets will always speak from a particular place and experience with Wisdom. Our mob say that you cannot speak to anyone beyond the tribe unless you have dwelled with the ancestors within the tribal boundaries of one's own given country. The universal, therefore, can never be heard except in the particular. There must be enfleshment, there must be embodiment, there must be language, culture and place or country. Without these, there can be no voice, not one that can be heard, anyway.

To what end, then, does Wisdom (or, as I would prefer to say, country) speak through elders and prophets? Well, Matthew 13:31–32 offers one way of answering this question:

> Jesus put before them another parable: "The kingdom of heaven is like a mustard seed that someone took and sowed in his field; it is the smallest of all the seeds, but when it has grown it is the greatest of shrubs and becomes a tree, so that the birds of the air come and make nests in its branches."

Now, as with most of the parables recorded in the Synoptic Gospels, Jesus is here taking something very familiar and making it less familiar, taking common wisdom and rendering it differently so that it becomes prophetic or counterintuitive. In this case, the trope of seed growing into a tree and the birds coming to settle into its branches is common wisdom, but the naming of the mustard seed as the smallest of seeds and its grown form as the largest of shrubs is not. For the mustard seed was certainly not the smallest of seeds in the ancient Near East nor was its mature form the "greatest" of shrubs.

2. See, for example, Moreton-Robinson, *Talkin' Up*.

So, something else is going on here, and I propose that it has something to do with the connection between the "kingdom of heaven"—the region, that is of the divine reign—and the birds of the air. Remember that earlier in Matthew's Gospel, in the homily known as the Sermon on the Mount, Jesus refers to the birds of the air as "they that neither sow nor reap nor gather into barns, and yet your heavenly Father feeds them" (Matt 6:26). In contrast to the citizens of the Roman Empire, who are encouraged by social and political convention to clothe themselves with the symbols of wealth and privilege, the birds of the air are fed and clothed by God. They do not sow or spin as a sign of their striving after a greater share of colonial power and largesse. Instead, they await the gratuity of the divine, universally given in creation for the sustenance of life.

So, whatever the size and greatness of the seed or the tree given by God, wherever it sits in the economies of colonial empire or the common wisdom, it is given simply to feed and to clothe those whom empire forgets—the lowly, the least, the communities who live close to the *humus* of the earth and depend upon her gratuity.

Thus, the kingdom of heaven is roughly analogous to country, as our mobs would understand it. She is given to all and for all. She gives herself for our feeding and clothing. Yet, because the gift is universally given, there is an implicit ethic to its use which resembles both the manna given to Israel in its wanderings and in the eucharist by which Christians are fed. We are to take only what is needed. We are not to hoard its fruit into barns for a rainy day or for the generating of surplus wealth. We are to take only what is needful for today. For she gives herself at great cost, the cost of life as it is poured out in death, so that all who eat of what is dead may themselves be sustained in life. As the Johannine Christ says, "Very truly, I tell you, unless a grain of wheat falls into the earth and dies, it remains just a single grain; but if it dies, it bears much fruit" (Jn 12:24).

As we noted in chapter 2, there are analogies between Indigenous notions of country and the Christian divine. I don't believe we can ever legitimately claim that one *is* the other in any literal one-to-one equivalence. What we can say, however, is that the realms of Wisdom and the kingdom of heaven are a lot like country. If we can therefore center ourselves in the home they create for us, rather than the little empires we would construct for ourselves against fear and chaos, we may well find that what is given us in country is enough; that the Voice we find in country and her prophets is enough. And perhaps we may finally, therefore, find the kind of justice that is able to make our broken humanity whole once more.

THE DOUBLE BIND OF THEOLOGICAL LANGUAGE

Here is another simple poem, this time from my own pen in 2020, about what Aboriginal people mean when we speak of country. It won't work for every Indigenous community, but I reckon it will resonate with most of us.

> We are all born from the watery womb of country;
> country feeds us with the pure nectar of her own life;
> from the beginning of creation, and in every moment, country dies;
> by her death, everything that is dead is made alive;
> country teaches us who we are, and how we are to live;
> country is our mother, our father, our uncle and aunty, our sister
>   and our brother;
> country is our kin, and in her familial body we find that all creation,
> plants, animals, even the stary host above, are kin to us as well;
> country teaches us to care for our kin as country cares for us;
> country bids us to imitate what we see in country,
> to watch, to listen, to imbibe and to notice,
> to take what we learn into ourselves and write it on our hearts;
> and when we die, country takes us into the heart of her own death
> that we may be born to an intimacy that is more wonderful than
>   anything we could think or imagine.

Perhaps you will have noticed some analogical similarities in that description with the way that Christians think about Christ? This leads me to conclude that "Christ" functions for Christian settlers as "country" functions for Aboriginal and Torres Strait Islander people. Precisely how these two realities are related is, of course, a very complex question for Christian theology. I don't want to detail the various models theologians have drawn up concerning the relationship between Christ and culture.[3] I only want to point out that they are, all of them, variations upon a simple double bind that seems permanently embedded in Christian tradition because of its Hebrew origins, namely: the Lord says, "represent me, but by no means represent me." This phrase is a shorthand way of saying that the God of the Bible both appears and disappears from human view and comprehension. On the one hand, Israel and the church are charged with representing

3. The reader may wish to consult Niebuhr, *Christ and Culture* or Regan and Torrance, *Christ and Context*.

the divine character and will, particularly thorough the material forms of liturgy and mission. On the other hand, Israel and the church are to honor the prohibition against the making of idols. They should never mistake their *representations* of the divine for the divine itself.[4]

There are two important implications of this fundamental structuring of reality as a double bind. On the one hand, none of us can step outside of our human traditions, texts, cultures, and landscapes in a manner which gives us a knowing access to a "God's-eye view" of it all. The God or the Christ who speaks to us cannot be heard except through the complex inter-actions between materiality, mind, tradition, and text we call culture. This is what Derrida meant by his famous aphorism: "there is nothing outside of the text."[5] On the other hand, all of us retain a sense that everything that we can know is conditioned or put in play by a mystery which can never be adequately known or represented by our cultures. Yet every cultural itera-tion somehow reaches for this mystery which never finally and compre-hensively presents itself. "Represent me, but by no means represent me."[6]

This means that it would be unwise to conclude that the "Christ" of Christians and the "country" of Aboriginal cosmology are identical. There may be analogical or family resemblances. But they are resemblances that we put in play, that we make. They do not, necessarily, represent or give adequate expression to what is "real." Conversely this means, also, that it would also be unwise to conclude that "Christ" and "country" are entirely unrelated realities, mutually exclusive symbolic models of the real which one must make an ultimate choice about. Most missionaries told our mobs that we must make a choice, that we should reject country, which is the devil, and embrace the colonial Christ. Some of us did as they asked, but most of us didn't.

It would be the height of arrogance to even attempt a European-styled taxonomy of what Aboriginal and Torres Strait Islander Christians believe about Christ in relation to country, even though that is precisely what I did in the last chapter. Because, except for those whose Indigenous selfhood has been almost entirely hollowed out by the relentless pressure of coloniza-tion, most Aboriginal Christians do, indeed, have a "both-and" rather than an "either-or" approach to the living of our lives. We are mostly disinclined

---

4. For the best meditation I have read on this double bind see Hart, *Trespass*.

5. Derrida, *Grammatology*, 158.

6. My own meditations on these phenomena were published as Deverell, *Bonds of Freedom*.

to compare, to measure and to quantify, to formulate and propose in the way that Europeans like to do. Most of us are entirely disinclined toward the metalanguage of European theology, which seeks to discern a kernel of continuity across the first-order narratives and rituals of a community, to more clearly (but rather abstractly) state what is true. For us, the truth lies closer to the earth, to our primary narratives and rituals. For us, theology of the European kind succeeds only to render the truth more abstract and disembodied.

Still, being a trawloolway man who has been (for good and for ill) trained in such dark arts, I will seek to outline what a *liturgical* Christology of country might look like, in broad outline. Be aware, as I do so, that what I mean by the term "liturgical Christology" is simply this: the coinherence of belief and practice such that what we believe about Christ can only be read from what we do, especially what we do in the embodied storytelling called ritual or ceremony. For an Aboriginal theology, this is the best way. For most of us are supremely impatient with more abstract forms of theology which appear, to us at least, entirely unconnected to the stories that we weave about real life.

CHRIST AS COUNTRY IN RITUAL AND LITURGICAL MODE

Broadly, ritual performs itself by binding together categories or dimensions of lived reality. These can be called time, space, body, and text. Let's examine the ways in which Aboriginal people and/or Torres Strait Islanders might render the relationship between Christ and country across each of these dimensions.

Let's begin with *time*.

For Indigenous people, time does not begin in the past, pass through a present, and orient itself towards a future. Time is a constant now, a present-continuous. Here there is a sense in which what Europeans call the "past" or a "future" can be experienced as a present. In ritual, therefore, even stories that apparently come from a distant past or an imagined future are understood to act upon the present to both maintain and create country. For the ancestors who created land and waterway, and continue to inhabit land and waterway, are forever creating land and waterway. They are the vitality which animates and sustains country in its aliveness. They are the presence which, at once, both traverses and ultimately suspends the very great distance between past and future. There may be resonances here with the Christian idea of an *eschaton* that bends past and future together into a present.[7] The biblical story that best represents that, from my point of view, is St. Mark's version of the transfiguration, where apparently dead ancestors speak with Jesus, whose future resurrection body is already apparently actualized in a present moment (Mk 9:2–10).

The implications of this perspective for a liturgical Aboriginal Christology would be at least twofold. First, the church year, with its narrative sense of movement from ancient promise through fleeting present and into a hoped-for but not-yet future fulfillment would probably need to make way for something more locally and presently discerned. Celebrations could be refocused on an ancestor Christ who, like the other Indigenous ancestors, presents himself in events that are at hand and concretely accessible in both space and time. One possibility for rearranging things might be to use local Indigenous seasons, which draw attention to the activity and movement of local flora and fauna, as potential analogues for telling Christ-as-country stories. So, to use the seasons of the East Kulin in Naarm/Melbourne, where I live, as an example,[8]

- Luk eel season (March), when the luk are fat and ready for harvesting and the binap (Manna gums) are flowering, could be a time when the fishing stories of the Gospels are told along with the stories of God's provision of manna and quail in the wilderness. There are connections here into Lenten stories of pilgrimage, grace, and surviving storms.

- Warring wombat season (April to July), when rainfall is at its highest, could be a time for telling the flood, water-crossing and baptismal stories of the Bible, particularly in relation to Easter. The warrings (wombats) who emerge during this time and forage close to the ground could become reminders of the humility of Christ, whose humility and humiliation bring him close to the ground, close to the earth, close to us. The unfurling of the fronds of the kombadik (soft tree fern) could be read as symbols of the unfurling of Christ and his mission through resurrection and the creation of the church at Pentecost.

- Guling orchid season (August), when guling and moyan (silver birch) flower, marks the beginning of the end of cooler temperatures. A time, possibly, for reflecting on the fruitfulness of the earth in relation to the

7. To my mind, the best elucidation of Christian eschatology in the European tradition remains Moltmann, *Way of Jesus.*

8. Bunjilaka Aboriginal Cultural Centre, "Eastern Kulin."

fruitfulness expected of the church, the vine of Christ. The star shape of the guling flower might occasion reflections on the way in which Christ shines like a star in the universe and calls the community of faith to do likewise.

- Poorneet tadpole season (September to October), when the poorneet fill the creeks, gurrborra (koalas) begin mating, and the pied currawongs call loudly to each other, can be a time to reflect more explicitly on the fertility or fruitfulness of country in relation to the fruit of the Spirit. The currawong might be taken as a kulin symbol of the go-between Spirit, as currawongs are legendary for their capacity to form friendships with other species, including humans.

- Buath gurru grass flowering season (November), when buarth gurru and corranderrk (Christmas bush) are flowering and the buliyong (bats) are feasting on insects, can be a time for continuing to reflect on the miracles of divine provision, and on the fruitfulness of discipleship. "Consider the lilies . . ." from the Sermon on the Mount.

- Kangaroo apple season (December), with its thundery, changeable weather, can be a time to reflect on the storms of faith and the fact that the divine presence can be hard to discern. There are connections here with Advent themes of waiting in darkness. Bundjil (the wedge-tailed eagle), who is a major creator ancestor for Kulin people, is breeding during this season. An opportunity to reflect upon the begetting of divine offspring, I'd suggest!

- Biderap dry season (January to February), when the heat kills many plants and the Southern Cross is high in the south at sunrise—a constellation which, in Kulin dreaming stories, is a resting place for Bundjil and two of his wives—could become a season for reflecting on the act of creation as a spiral of death and rebirth by which country/Christ gives itself in death in order to guarantee that life will continue.

I share these seasonal suggestions very much as a for-instance rather than as a definitive template. The reader is encouraged to investigate the seasonal spirals and flows known by mob where you live and apply a bit of liturgical creativity to what is given in the living dynamism of that landscape.

A second implication of this Indigenous sense of time is a recognition that the movement of the Sunday liturgy need not be sequenced as gathering/word/meal/sending, whatever that order's pedigree in first- and second-century Middle Eastern Christianity. For Indigenous people, these moments all coinhere and therefore the precise order in which things happen is not so important (including when to turn up and when to leave). What is important to Indigenous people is not *when* they happen, only *that* they happen. It is important to gather in community, even if not everyone is present at precisely the same time. It is important to listen to the foundational stories of the community, but these can be heard, told, and performed in myriad ways across and through a gathering event. It is important that food be shared, for in the sharing of food a community is sustained in the crucial practice of reciprocal giving and receiving, which is at the heart of any community's survival. But the eating can begin straight away. And it can happen as the stories are being told. And it can continue as surplus food is taken to those who are sick or absent, for whatever reason— surely a bedrock practice of missional sending, which is also important. The stories need to be told, and the food needs to be shared, beyond any precise gathering of the community. For the stories themselves ask that of us. They ask that the ethical perspectives embedded in the stories becomes flesh in every place that a representative of the community travels. They ask that representatives of the gathered community also learn to recognize and read those stories in the people, land, skyscapes, and waterscapes all about. But this does not mean that the community ceases to be gathered as people move in and out of the circle. In larger perspective, any gathering is a cosmic gathering, a community of being which includes all created life. This means that it is quite impossible to go anyplace which is somehow "beyond" the kinship system of being. Every travelling pilgrim will simply return to a place they never left, and perhaps know it anew.[9]

But I am already talking about a second dimension of ceremony or liturgy: space. Or, better, *place.*

For Indigenous people, place (and, by implication, space) is a more important organizing dimension of reality than "time." Place, the part of the world to which you belong by virtue of being kin with the ancestors who inhabit that place, is the most fundamental determinant of identity, belonging, and responsibility. When Indigenous people walk or swim or sail our boats on the country and waterways to which we belong, it is as if we are walking and swimming or sailing across the bodies of our creator ancestors. We hear their call and attend to our responsibilities to care for

---

9. I'm paraphrasing T. S. Eliot in "Little Gidding." See Eliot, *Four Quartets.*

those places, including the plants and animals that live there along with people. All are our kin. In this perspective, Jesus may be understood as kin too, perhaps one of the ancestors who make and indwell country. After all, a great deal of his recorded teaching involves lessons gleaned from the non-human world. A mustard seed, a tree, a field, the birds of the air, for instance.

The implications of this perspective for a liturgical Christology would be at least fourfold. First, the physical environment in which we worship should, at least, closely resemble the land and waterscape that is important to the local custodians. If a building is really necessary, make it as open to the smells and sights and sounds of that place as possible. Reduce the prevalence of the markers or barriers between "inside" and "outside." Dissolve the thresholds. For Christ-as-country is communicating through these things at least as much as through the objects and artifacts derived from a European heritage.

Second, you might also consider bringing the outside inside by designing furniture, vestments, vessels, and openings in such a way that they draw on the imagery of local landscapes. Consider the ways in which analogical links might be made between biblical images of God in Christ and local landscapes. Let the baptismal pool be an actual pool. And let it be fed from a creek. Let the altar be as gnarled as an old tree but with a contoured surface, evoking the old covenant and the new, the passion and the resurrection. Let the ambo or lectern stand upon a sculpture of the most important creator ancestor. We already, in some traditions, sculpt lecterns in the shape of eagles. Let's just extend that notion to other local ancestors.

Third, I would also challenge you to remove imagery that preserves nothing other than a colonial imagination regarding white supremacy. Like representations of Jesus and the apostles that have exclusively blonde hair and blue eyes. Like the Bishop Tyrell window at St. James' in Morpeth, that has an all-white cast at the Last Supper, except for Judas, who is black. Spaces that embed and proclaim such ideology will be difficult places for Indigenous people to step into, for the buildings themselves cry out against us.

Finally, I would encourage the reader to think about worshipping in such a way that the people gathered face each other for much of the celebration, as primary sacraments of country-as-Christ, rather than persisting with the model of imperial courts that we inherited from Rome in which the people face the backs of their fellow worshippers most of the time, with the priestly class, the choir, and the holy symbols being significantly closer to God than the people are. Let the holy things be in the midst of the holy people. Let them take their place in a circle of worshippers which mirrors the spiralling nature of the cosmos represented in Indigenous art. For circles are about communities in which everyone shares, equally, in the community's capacity to resound with divinity and become a portal or icon of divine presence. Circles are also about the eternal return of life after death or, better, life through death. In that sense, they are a far better icon of both country and the paschal mystery of Christians than a magisterial court ever was!

Let's talk now about *body*, or *materiality*.

For Indigenous people, as I have already indicated, your body does not belong to you alone. For you are part of a community that includes not only the other people who belong to your country, but also the plants, the animals, the waterways, and the landscape itself. You even belong to the stars above, a heavenly body that mirrors, according to many dreaming stories, the way things are below. If we take a Christ-as-country perspective, then Christ's body includes not only word, bread, wine, baptismal water, and the people of God. It also includes, as the apostle to the Colossians says, the whole created order (Col 1:15–20).[10]

The implications for an Aboriginal liturgical Christology are fourfold. First, let food continue to be the primary sacrament, the primary symbol of Christ-as-country. For in both traditions, if they are taken to be distinct, food is the primary sign of divine care, given through death and dying to keep us alive and living. But let us not be bound by the European insistence on bread and wine. I would argue that these are symbols of Christ's body and blood only because they were staple food and drink in the culture in which Jesus lived and the church was born. They might be at least partially replaced in other cultures by other staples. In a great many Aboriginal cultures, the staple "bread" is a yam, and the staple "wine" just the tannin-stained water drawn from a complex network of creeks which, in Aboriginal cosmology, is like the veins of country, how country distributes its lifeblood to the whole body.

Second, as I intimated above, let the community of people itself, rather than a clerical class, become primary symbols of Christ-as-country. This can be expressed in the ritual context not only by the spatiality of

___

10. To my mind, the classic Western work on this concept remains McFague, *Body of God.*

facing each other, as I have already said, but also by a more regular and active participation of the whole community in what is said and done. In Aboriginal society there is no simple distinction between the priestly class and the people, especially in the performance of ritual. Yes, certain elders have responsibility for bringing people together to design, rehearse, and perform the rituals. And their experience and knowledge with the dreaming is taken seriously as genuine wisdom. But this acknowledged authority only rarely translates into ritual performances in which elders do most of the work. They are more like directors or choreographers who work with people beforehand so that they will be ready to participate and to take their part in what will unfold. Some of you will argue that this is what clergy are supposed to be in an authentic Christianity as well. That may well be true in theory. I hope it is true! It's just that in all my years of ecumenical wandering, I've rarely seen it happen in practice.

Third, I've already talked about the ways in which the Christ-body that is country can inhabit the liturgical space of our buildings. What I would add to that is a careful attention not only to visual arts and media, but also to the senses of hearing, smell, taste, and touch. If the doors and windows are not there, or at least wide open to country, the smells of country can make their way into the space, and many of those smells are associated with the way in which country dies to maintain its life. Surely a passion play in olfactory mode. The sounds of country can also intrude. The song of birds giving praise. The breezes in the trees, like ancestral spirits or a Holy Spirit, connecting and communicating. The movement of tides, with their missional movements of gathering and dispersal, and their echoes of labor and childbirth. The sound of rain, lifeblood to bring dead seeds to life and grow in trees like Christ being raised to shelter all creation. And so on. This is territory for poets!

Which brings us, finally, to possibly the least important part of the whole mix—*texts*.

For Indigenous people, written texts are not at all part of the way in which wisdom was passed on from generation to generation. Wisdom was passed on by conversation, by a great deal of behavioral modelling, and by ritual storytelling. You know, dancing, singing, and all that. Ceremony. For us, the primary "text" is country itself. The stories that tell us who we are, to whom we belong, and what we are responsible for is written there. The land speaks, but in a voice far more multilayered than even the greatest of human choirs could hope to produce. Country even speaks with a voice that sounds very similar to that of the Christ who lives and dies and lives again to give us, as human creatures who participate in his gratuity, that very same life and death and life again. I've hinted at that analogy often, along the way. So, what relationship can there be between the text that is country and written, liturgical texts? Well, quite a lot.

It is important to remember that the primary text of Christians, the Bible, and the texts which were slowly and painstakingly created as aids to the ritual performances of its message, have their origins in an oral and ritual tradition which did not, overall, involve the use of written texts at all. Traditions, stories, and rituals were remembered and passed on orally and kinaesthetically. Except in time of crisis, when communities were being pulled apart and the possibility of oral transmission was at risk. Like in the exile to Babylon. Like when Jerusalem was being destroyed by the Romans, and Christians needed to scatter to the four winds. The Bible is therefore marked by orality in the way that it preserves conversations and arguments between different schools of thought, in the way that it preserves multiple versions of the same stories that are ever-so-slightly different to each other, and in the way it preserves stories which were clearly bodily performances before they were texts. And the earliest surviving liturgical texts of the church are—by modern standards—extremely minimalistic. They assume that the local community has a great many prayers and stories and rituals already committed to memory.

Written liturgical texts which were expanded and printed so that people could read them in church obviously only arrived very late to the cause. Their prevalence and scope grew in proportion to the literacy of the people of God, first with many monastics and clergy, and later with the larger part of the people of God. At least in Western Europe and its colonies. At least amongst white people.

In much, but not all, of the white European world, a dependence on written texts which are made available to everyone, has almost completely replaced orality. This means that rituals have come to depend more upon reading and less upon creative or dramatic storytelling and memorized dialogue. It also means that liturgical texts tend to be created at some distance from the language, culture, and local lifeworlds of the people who end up using them. Thus, going to church has become more of a "head" activity than a body and heart activity, particularly in churches where the liturgy is newly created every week and is therefore all the more dependent upon the capacity of the congregation to read a single language. In these churches, remembered prayers and ritual actions are of little use and those who cannot read are almost entirely excluded. In a world where novelty is king, there is little call for such things.

So, what does this mean for an Aboriginal liturgical Christology? It means, first, that when the Christian tradition speaks of Christ as the word of God made flesh it is using a metaphor. In the Hebrew tradition, somewhat paradoxically, the word of God is usually and habitually oral. Yes, some of it was written down in moments of national crisis, but the written text was never supposed to supplant oral and ritual transmission. Not for Christians either. The word of God, in Christian tradition, is primarily a person, Jesus Christ, who lives and communicates through multiple means, including parables, and whose life, death, and resurrection might then be interpreted as, itself, a parable. Books, in other words, especially books of liturgical rites, should never be mistaken for the law or word of God. "The letter kills, the spirit gives life," said St. Paul (2 Cor 3:6).

Second, there is a great deal to be learned from oral cultures like those of more intact and stable Aboriginal and Torres Strait Islander cultures which, at the same time, have wonderful memories for rituals but rarely feel the need to freeze them in written texts. The word of life is living. It is ever old and ever new: old like the stories of creator ancestors, and new because those stories can be told repeatedly but a little differently each time, to address the needs of the community as it stands right now. So let us learn from the Bible and let us tell its stories. But must there be such a hard-and-fast division between the reading of Scripture and the preaching? Can't the preaching include a retelling of the stories, retellings that already address the community?

Third, if there must be written prayers, let them be more poetic and open to slippages in meaning. Let them lack the precision of this paper, let them leave room for interpretation. And let them be performed, and not merely read. Let them be adequately prepared. If there must be written prayers, let them speak of God and of Christ using the language of country. Let them refer to sights and sounds and smells and a sense of place that is locally capable of speaking about Christ.

And finally, let there remain large sections of the liturgy that are committed to memory by the whole community. A memorialization not only of word, but also of action, so that all for whom the written text is inaccessible by dint of education or culture, can still participate.

CHAPTER 4

Country, Jeremiah, and the Ecological Crisis[1]

TWO SACRED BOOKS

As a child I was very talkative. At the edge of the vast estates of barley, wheat, and potatoes which dominated the landscape where we lived, were small stands of native bush: atop hills, on the steep slopes of mountains, and along creeks. Whenever the opportunity arose, this is where I would wander. And as I wandered, I would talk. Not with myself (though many might see it that way) but with the trees and the ferns, the crows and the hawks, the wallabies, and the potoroos, even the rocks and the waterfalls, that I passed on my way. I would greet them all cheerfully and enquire about what kind of day each was having. I would pause to watch and to listen a while, finally wishing each well and offering a prayer or an incantation seeking their good and their well-being. Sometimes I would tell them about me, my troubles, my hopes, my bewilderments. And I would hear their voices speaking back to me. Not in English, mind. Whatever the language, however, I understood. I heard wisdom. I heard care. I heard guidance. And, after a little while, I would return to my family, my school, and all the complex negotiations of civilized life, somehow calmed and refreshed.

As a teenager, another conversation partner was added. The Bible. I became fascinated with its characters and voices, as many and as varied as

1. This chapter grew from two sources. The first was a homily preached at Christ Church, South Yarra, during Lent of 2021. The second is a published article: Deverell, "Bushfires."

I knew in the bush, though considerably more violent. Here were people I recognized. People who suffered great injustice, whose hopes and dreams were shattered. People who stole, raped, murdered, and committed genocide to obtain what belonged to another people. People who were afraid, but who were able to overcome their fears through faith in God. People who were able to change their hearts and their behavior because they believed in the mercy of God. People who carried great wounds and flaws, and yet were chosen to become God's emissaries. These days I marvel that a book as violent and as tragic a testament to our inhumanity towards one another as ever was written, could simultaneously bear a message from and about a God of love. But it does. On every page. For what the Bible finally proclaims, surely, is this: first, that we are loved by God, even as we fail, consistently and repeatedly, to love each other; and second, that because God has not given up on us, it is possible not only to recognize and learn such love, but also to abide in its mysterious power more deeply and consistently.

So, two conversation partners, two sources of wisdom for the living of life as a trawloolway man who is also a Christian. The one located in a sacred book, a book brought to this country by the colonizer, and the other located in a sacred landscape, a landscape that is alive with the presence of ancestor spirits who can be spoken to, and who can speak. Both book and country, in their own ways, are sacred texts. Both, being full of divine spirit, may be consulted for wisdom and guidance, if you know how. If I have a lament, today, it is not that the colonizer has attended carefully to the sacred book, and not enough to sacred country. No, my lament is more comprehensive, that the colonizer has paid little attention to either.

Here I want to draw your attention to the second chapter of Jeremiah which says, in part:

> Thus says the Lord:
> I remember the devotion of your youth,
>   your love as a bride,
> how you followed me in the wilderness,
>   in a land not sown.
> What wrong did your ancestors find in me
>   that they went far from me,
>
> and went after worthless things, and became worthless themselves?
> I brought you into a plentiful land
>   to eat its fruits and its good things.

But when you entered you defiled my land,
    and made my heritage an abomination.

The priests did not say, "Where is the Lord?"
Those who handle the law did not know me;
    the rulers transgressed against me.

Be appalled, O heavens, at this,
    be shocked, be utterly desolate,
    says the Lord,
for my people have committed two evils:
    they have forsaken me,
    the fountain of living water,
    and dug out cisterns for themselves,
cracked cisterns
    that can hold no water. (Jer 2:2b, 5, 7, 8, 12, 13)

This oracle, first uttered in the presence of the last king of Judah, is uncannily prescient about where we find ourselves, right now, as a nation and as a church. It is true, is it not, that we have forgotten the ancient ways, the ways here described as a covenant, a marriage, a communion with the divine in the wild places, a country not sown or intensively cultivated. Is it not true, as the prophet says, that upon entering this country the colonists saw the land not as a cathedral in which the divine might be known and worshipped, but rather as a commodity to be exploited in exchange for wealth and influence? Did not the colonists clear the land of its sovereign owners and managers, its first peoples, in a manner that fundamentally fractured the terms of God's law and covenant? Did they not covet what belonged to their neighbors, did they not steal and rape and murder to obtain what they desired? Does not that theft, rape, and murder continue to this day? Is not the lament of those of us who have survived that genocide also the lament of the land itself, and the ancestor spirits who dwell therein, and of God's own self? Are we not, Aboriginal and Torres Strait Islander peoples, the voice of the crucified one who is, at one and the same time, both country and Christ?

By commodifying this country and removing those whom the divine Spirit placed here to manage and cultivate its fruitfulness, colonists have polluted the sacred stream our creator ancestors provided for all of us as a gift, the stream of sacred lore designed to sustain us in life over many hundreds of millennia. Instead, we have dug cisterns for ourselves, cisterns so badly designed that they can barely hold water: practices and structures and policies which have brought us to point of ecological emergency, and to the certainty of a fundamental implosion in the ecological operating system of our planet. Unless. Unless we repent of our sin. Unless we turn again to the divine whose wisdom and way may be discerned in both sacred text and sacred country.

BUSHFIRES AND COLONIAL MISMANAGEMENT OF ABORIGINAL LANDS

The Australian bushfires that raged from September 2019 to February 2020 were the most destructive on record, claiming twelve million hectares of bush, farmland, town, and residential country in the states of New South Wales, Victoria, and South Australia. If that number is hard to get your head around, think of an area the size of the Canadian provinces of Nova Scotia and Prince Edward Island combined, then double it. In some places, the fires burned so hot that stone structures melted and even the biomatter below the surface of the ground was utterly obliterated. Ecologists are now saying that in such places, nothing will ever be able to grow again. Even where this is not the case, in parts of the forest where regeneration is possible, whole ecosystems—millennia in the making—have been utterly laid to waste. It is also estimated that over one billion native animals perished in the fires, many of them belonging to species already close to extinction, such as koalas and mountain pygmy possums. A large portion of those animals apparently died either because the fires were travelling too fast or because they could not make their way through the fences erected by property owners.[2]

So how did the fires start and why did they burn so hot? The short answer is that the continent of Australia is on the front line of the battle over climate change. Increasingly mild "cold" seasons and increasingly hot "warm" seasons over the past thirty years have left the driest continent on earth (after Antarctica) even drier. Periods of drought, always an issue in this sunburnt continent, have become progressively more severe over time to the point where even the wettest places on the continent—temperate and tropical rainforests—are becoming tinderboxes. When dry lightning comes along, therefore, there is little to stop entire forests, along with any farms and towns on their perimeter, going up in flames. And once the fires start, even the world's most prepared and well-resourced firefighting services

2. These statistics are taken from Wheeling, "Most Extreme."

cannot stand in their way. There is little to be done except to evacuate residential areas and pray for rain.

But how did we get to this point? How did an apparently "developed" nation such as Australia allow the situation to get so out of hand, possibly to the point of no return? Obviously, climate change is a global issue. Even if Australia had progressive governments that take climate change seriously (which it does not) the only possible mechanism that will make a difference to global policy is international treaty. And the world's largest polluters have not yet signed any of the protocols generated by UN conferences such as Kyoto or Paris. Notwithstanding this fact, I believe it is incumbent upon nations such as Australia to recognize that we find ourselves in these catastrophic circumstances primarily because we have failed to recognize the wisdom of our Indigenous peoples.

I am an Indigenous survivor of what some of us are calling, in Australia, "the apocalypse."[3] Before the British arrived on our shores in 1788, over three hundred nations were already living here, and we had done so since creation.[4] When you've been in a place for that long, you get to know it very, very, very well. You get to know the moods and cycles of land and seascape. You get to know the seasons, the animals, the plant life, and how they all interact with each other. You get to know the ecological systems which bind that land together and cause it to flourish with life. You get to know how to find food and shelter, and how to sustainably access those resources over many hundreds of generations. The other thing that you do when you've lived that long in one place is find a way to preserve the knowledge of previous generations and pass it onto your children. Doing so is crucial to survival. My people preserved our wisdom in a large body of knowledge we now call, collectively, our "dreaming." It consists of songs, dances, paintings, stories, and rituals which, together, amount to a primordial sense of patterning to the cosmos showing us how to live successfully and well in the lands and waterways we call home. When the British arrived, they apparently did not see the value of our lore—indeed, after only a little while, they devised policies and practices specifically designed to destroy it—and this was the beginning of our apocalypse. During the 235 years of British occupation a great deal of our lore has been destroyed and

---

3. Abbatangelo, "Apocalypse." See also a speech I gave to the 2019 Synod of the Anglican Diocese of Melbourne: Deverell, "Garry's Speech."

4. For those who are more inclined to believe scientists than dreaming stories, an archaeological dig near Warrnambool in Victoria is estimating that human beings have lived there for one hundred and ten thousand years. See Sherwood, "Moyjil Site."

possibly lost for ever. Certainly, we have been systematically murdered or separated from the specific places in which our various dreamings belong. And that has meant, worst of all, that most of us are no longer able to fulfill the vocation given us by our creator ancestors to look after and manage our homes in such a way that future generations may continue to enjoy and live from their bounty.

Of the many skills our ancestors learned and passed on was the management of landscapes and resources through fire farming. When the British arrived, they moved into the land based on a fiction that the land was "virgin," empty of truly human presence, cultivation, and influence. This is now known as the legal doctrine of *terra nullius*. Of course, the doctrine was false. For thousands upon thousands of years, my people had been modifying the landscape on an epic scale. We had been using fire to create agricultural fields in which we could plant crops, fields where the soil was permeable by both air and water. We had been using fire to create grasslands which would attract game which could then, in turn, be harvested.[5] Crucially, for the current discussion, we also set small, "cold" fires to prevent "hot" wildfires that were likely to get out of control and destroy whole ecosystems. These would be set, on a seasonal basis, within large stands of trees as well as in open grasslands. The fires would be managed by burning small areas in a circle-pattern, with a large group of people lighting fires at the center and then following the fire out into a widening perimeter. Circle burning allows you to keep control of a fire and keep it contained. It also allows the animals that live on that country to move on for a while, until the fire is done, and country begins to regenerate. Many of Australia's native plant species require fire to regenerate and therefore provide nourishment for local ecosystems to survive.[6]

By contrast, the British had very little clue about how to manage our lands sustainably. Within the first fifty years of annexation, they cleared the grasslands of its people, agricultural systems, and animals, and replaced them with millions upon millions of cattle and sheep which compacted the soil and made it relatively impermeable to air and water. The soil, which could no longer breathe, became progressively less nutritious over time and, when it rained, less able to hold moisture. More grasslands for sheep

5. Two of the more accessible texts exploring these practices are Pascoe, *Dark Emu*, and Gamage, *Biggest Estate*.

6. Fire-farming knowledge has been beautifully preserved in the Firesticks program started by Victor Steffensen and his father, Tommy George. You can read their story in Steffensen, *Fire Country*.

and cattle were created by cutting down forests, but those stands that remained were poorly managed so that wild, out-of-control bushfires became a feature of the Australian experience. Today's Australia not only has to contend with wildfires, but also with deeply unwell river systems, dying coral reefs and fisheries, alarming levels of drought and desertification, as well as one of the world's most mismanaged native animal populations. According to the Ecological Society of Australia, over one hundred species of animal have become entirely extinct since European colonization began, and over eighteen hundred are listed as in danger of extinction.[7]

Some policymakers are becoming interested in the land and sea management practices of First Peoples. But they are few and far between. And so, we pray to our creators for mercy, and for a change of heart and mind that can reverse at least some of the damage. And we do so, some of us, in the name of the one who loved even the lilies of the field.

In the world of politics and public policy, better management of country will require removing the puppets of capitalism from government and replacing them with people who are willing to listen to the still, small, voice of the divine Spirit. In our churches it will mean exorcising all that remains of that possessive, status-hungry, exclusionary impulse and replacing it with the disciplines of listening, hospitality, and prophecy. For unless the voices we generally exclude, ignore, and belittle are welcomed to the table, then we shall be as guilty of killing the prophets and dancing on their graves as the kings of Israel and the priests of its temple. And we shall pay for it in the end by finding ourselves at the wrong end of the *Magnificat*: scattered to the bottom of the food chain, empty, nothing.

All of which is to offer an invitation to the reader. See, I place before you the way that leads to death and the way that leads to life. If you die to your self-importance, and the self-importance of the colonial imagination, you will be empty enough for the divine spirit to fill you with life. But if you hang onto such things, you will find that you are already dead. And your deadness will continue to infect the systems and networks of which you are part, both publicly and privately. As the spiral of Lent into Easter is properly a return to the waters of baptism, to receive there, through repentance and the death of self, the risen life of Christ; so may you also turn to the rivers and creeks of country, through which the divine voice of country speaks a word of grace that will renew not only your own life, but also our churches and communities, and the life of the whole planetary ecosystem.

7. Ecological Society of Australia, "Australia's Species."

To that end, I offer this prayer to my settler friends, for use in this time of ecological catastrophe.

God of Jesus Christ
we come to you because there is nowhere else to turn.
There is a famine in our land,
a famine of living and telling the truth.

We confess that we invaded this land and enslaved its peoples,
the people who have cared for this country and its waterways
for thousands upon thousands of years.

We confess that we have wilfully ignored the wisdom of the First
Peoples,
wisdom about how to live in this country in a way that honors and
preserves all life,
that we have trampled their knowledge underfoot and treated it
with contempt.

We confess that we have treated the land itself with contempt,
and its seas and waterways also.
We have not cared for it as we ought to have done.
Instead, we have exploited and raped it to feed our selfish appetites.

Now the land is sick.
It weeps and cries out in pain.
Its plants and animals, the rich tapestry of its ecosystems,
are burning up for lack of nourishment and care.
And it is our fault.

Teach us, O God, to amend both our lives
and the political and economic systems in which they are embedded.
Teach us to treasure the First Nations of this land
and their wisdom about how to live here with respect and sensitivity.
Teach us to treasure the country and waterways on which we
depend,
its cycles and seasons, its plants and animals, its fragile and
beautiful ecosystems.
Teach us to call our political leaders to account.
Teach us, O God, to live and tell the truth.

God of Jesus Christ,
We come to you because there is nowhere else to turn.
Have mercy on us and free us from our sins.
Amen.

Chapter 5

Contemplation on Colonized Country

ON MIRIAM-ROSE UNGUNMERR-BAUMANN'S "DADIRRI"

Colonization is not only about the annexation of land and the removal of those who live on it. It is also about the annexation and repurposing of imagination and thought. The "white possessive" (a term from Aileen Moreton-Robinson) wants to own the brains and hearts of Indigenous peoples, as well as our territories and bodies.[1] That is why the "welcome" offered to Indigenous people into white institutions, especially institutions of learning, is deeply conditional. "You are welcome" means "You are welcome so long as you submit to our (white) social imagination, our (white) epistemologies and our (white) ontologies." Resisting the terms of that conditional welcome is fraught with difficulty because it is offered by the dominant, controlling culture. It is a welcome backed not only institutional power, but also by the dominant social imaginary that animates that power. In this context, when a white teacher says, "listen to me," the invitation comes with a number of unspoken corollaries: "because I know the objective truth . . . because your truth is inadequate in the white world you must face . . . because your survival as a worthwhile contributor to (colonial) society depends upon your listening . . ." and so on.

1. Moreton-Robinson, *White Possessive*.

Miriam-Rose Ungunmerr-Baumann's invitation to come listen ("dadirri") to country is deeply radical, and therefore easily misunderstood.[2] She is not inviting settlers into a lovely, wafty spiritual experience with "nature," for example, the kind of experience that you can also get from a Western Buddhism that is compatible with, and supportive of, white middle-class suburban life. She is inviting settlers to question and relativize the very foundations of the white possessive, including its imaginative power, its epistemologies, and ontologies. What Miriam-Rose means by "dadirri" is a deep and sustained process of conversion, of learning and unlearning: a learning about Indigenous practices of ethical relationality with the creator ancestors who formed the earth, with country and waterway, with animals and plants, and finally with other people; and, with that, a subsequent unlearning of settler practices that ignore and even abuse these deeply beloved kin.

Conversion like this will certainly never happen if Indigenous knowledges and practices continue to be seen as interesting but exotic and marginal: pretty and decorative, like a dot painting on the wall of a suburban home that is otherwise entirely European in style. Conversion only comes, I believe, when the stability and apparent "success" of a particular paradigm starts to come undone. Many of us hope that the ecological emergency that is slowly starting to penetrate even white Western consciousness, in tandem with the collapse and imminent implosion of settler churches and their supporting theologies, may create the kind of crisis in which Christian settlers will eventually turn to what the world's oldest living cultures might have to contribute.

Insofar as the Christian faith can be an ally in that learning and unlearning, Miriam-Rose, myself, and many others are happy to be identified as Christian. But the Christian faith we embrace will be necessarily different from settler ways of being Christian. Our Indigenous faith remembers that Christianity arose in a colonial setting as a protest against the excesses of the Roman Empire and against the Jewish leaders who collaborated with empire in their oppression of ordinary people. Our faith remembers that Jesus was a keen observer of the processes and cycles of local ecosystems, and that he counselled his hearers to attend to the lessons he observed there in the parables. Our faith remembers that Jesus blurred the difference between bread and his body, wine and his blood, all these things being, for him, a dying and a mourning by which life and joy is given anew, as much

---

2. Ungunmerr, "Dadirri."

in country and ecosystem as in human community. Our faith remembers that Jesus was concerned, most of all, with the last and the least, the forgotten victims of oppressive structures and regimes. In him we see ourselves, and we hear in his message the voice of our creator ancestors who say that life is not yet spent, that there is hope yet for a better tomorrow.

CONTEMPLATION AS SOVEREIGNTY AND JOY

To speak of hope is, of course, a deeply controversial move in Aboriginal Australia. Chelsea Watego, for example, says that hope is not a luxury that most colonized peoples can afford:

> Hope to me has always worked for the folks for whom everything turns up trumps, through whatever adversity they meet. Hope was never for the hopeless. It was always the stuff of fairy tales and fables, which were reserved exclusively for white people and, occasionally, those respectable ethnics.[3]

According to Watego, hope is a tool of the oppressor. It is part of a carefully designed strategy for keeping black people in our place:

> But this is the function of hope in a colonial-settler state. Like role models, capacity-building agendas, reconciliation action plans and an Indigenousness derived from nowhere, hope offers up change without change. This is why colonisers are so insistent we have it—hope is not an enabler of our existence, but of theirs. It is not a vehicle of Black emancipation —it is a psychological tool of the coloniser to insist that we accept things the way they are, forevermore . . . Retiring hope is to relinquish having hope in colonial institutions predicated upon our non-existence. If we take nihilism as our starting point, maybe we will be more strategic with the sacrifices we are prepared to make, and demand more from those we once invested our hopes in.

I cannot disagree, especially as a theologian of country. For if the primary source of our spiritual health, as Indigenous people, is country, what are we to do if we cannot get meaningful access to our country? What are we to do if there is literally zero chance that most of us will ever walk upon country again, because most of our land and waterways are now in the hands of government, corporations, and private citizens? Some might

3. Watego, *Another Day*, 190.

say, "Well, what about native title legislation? Won't that deliver what you need?" Not really. For native title legislation, in most instances, succeeds in giving only a small fraction of the Indigenous population "access" to an equally small fraction of what was once ours. Most of our country remains in the hands of others. And "access" is not the same as living with and from country. Access cannot deliver a spiritual indwelling with country, a mutual caring with country, an economic, social, and cosmic sense of belonging in country. Access cannot deliver what Aboriginal people really need to not only survive but thrive. For access does not allow us to learn from country, in the deep and abiding way our ancestors did and, out of that learning, care for country in ways which make for health and well-being for every creature that lives there.

The push for sovereignty is not only about property rights, but it certainly includes them. If you have no control over who interacts with country, and how, then the health of country cannot be guaranteed. And if country suffers, so do we who depend upon country for our well-being and spiritual health. For country is our sacred text. From it we read who we are, to whom we belong, and what our vocation or responsibilities are. If we cannot live in, and from, country, then we approach our lives without the kind of spiritual guidance that Holy Scripture gives to people who hold these sacred. If we cannot hope for country's return, then we cannot hope. That is what Watego is really trying to say. And she is right.

What, then, is the alternative to hope if, as Watego argues, everything that hope pins itself to can never be delivered under our colonial system? Her own answer is twofold: "Be sovereign" and "be joyful." For Watego, sovereignty is about committing oneself to a framework that is no longer dependent upon the colonial imagination and the crumbs that may (or may not) fall from the master's table. It is to embrace a "black nihilism" that places its faith and hope only in black people, black communities, black thinking, and black action:

> Black nihilism, in all of its supposed hopelessness, means an existence framed on our terms, and not on our non-existence. It means freeing up that wasted time to attend to things that matter to us first, and refusing to be of service to the coloniser and their things. Black nihilism in all of its supposed ugliness is also the place in which I have found joy, a joy more rewarding than those occasional blue-sky moments. There is much possibility in this place for a sovereignty that is embodied and enacted by us and

> there is a joy in theorising sovereignty as survival in the everyday,
> as opposed to clinging to white hope and Black hopelessness.[4]

So, to be clear, what Watego is arguing for, here, is not a doing away with hope altogether, but rather a refocusing of hope on regions—people and modes of thinking—outside the colonial project: Indigenous sovereignty, Indigenous thinking, Indigenous action. To my theological mind, this is a version of the *via negativa* espoused by the Jewish and Christian mystics. One must let go of "god" to discover "God." One must be done with idols, which are just phantasms and mind games designed to distract us from what is important, to embrace the Real. One must abandon one's hope in merely human institutions and human solutions—infected as they are by the lust for illegitimate power—to enable a hearing and an understanding of what the divine is really calling us to. And so on.

So, to put it another way, a theological version of Watego's thesis might seek to deconstruct the coloniality of a theology which forever promises the poor and oppressed "heaven" without ever lifting a finger to make that happen in our present reality. And it might do so in the name of a divinity which has already given us "heaven" in the form of country and therefore has no need for the category of an infinitely deferred and deferring "promised land." Some might dismiss this as an overly "realized" eschatology, and I'm fine with that. So be it. Indigenous people cannot afford the luxury of constructing any heaven except this marvellously fecund earth, given us in country and each other. Nor do we have any use for the threat of "hell" because hell is here already, created by greedy people who want to possess and consume the world and everyone in it. Confronted with the fact of human evil, we are inclined to fight, to resist, to deploy every conceivable non-violent means, to take back that which has been stolen. For the only time meaningful to Indigenous people is the eventfulness of now, and the only "angels" we can depend on are ourselves and the ancestral powers who speak through country.

This is to take us back to an ontology that prioritizes place over time. The divine is not, primarily, to be found in a promised future that may never arrive. The deferral of divine arrival is a messianic fiction that does little else but legitimate the deferral of justice for Indigenous people. Rather, for us, the divine must be understood as that which gives itself in the dirt beneath our feet and in the plants, animals, and people all around. If we are to place our hope in anything, it is in the iconography of what is already

4. Watego, *Another Day*, 214.

given in country. That means that our struggles for a real and meaningful sovereignty and the preservation of what remains of country are very much about the here and now. What we do now to prosecute that struggle has genuinely cosmic implications. We cannot depend on the "get out of jail free" card of a promised saviour who will arrive, as it were, from another planet to undo all the misery we have made for ourselves. The saviour, if she is anywhere, is in this place, in country: in its awe-inspiring holiness and in its resilience, despite everything we throw at her. The saviour is also in every action, thought, and feeling that bends towards justice for country and her stewards. Joy is therefore to be found not by hoping for a magical solution that takes little account of the colonial realities with which we must contend, but in each moment, each action, every moment of consciousness that is able to create an imaginative space between what is given in country and the colonial project. In this is a contemplative practice born not from future-oriented hope, but from being firmly and radically rooted, like a tree, in the place where our ancestors dwell, drawing on their strength and their guidance to sustain us in the struggle.

"WAIT WITHOUT HOPE"

In "East Coker" (1940), the second of his *Four Quartets*, T. S. Eliot wrote this:

> I said to my soul, be still, and wait without hope
> For hope would be hope for the wrong thing; wait without love,
> For love would be love of the wrong thing; there is yet faith
> But the faith the love and the hope are all in the waiting.
> Wait without thought, for you are not ready for thought:
> So the darkness shall be the light, and the stillness the dancing.[5]

Here Eliot names what is essential, I believe, to the apprehension of genuine contemplatives, whether they be Christian or more anciently Aboriginal in their ontology or phenomenology of expression. What Eliot names here is the interruption, the breaking, the ending, or even the impossibility, of everyday life. For everyday life is indeed broken, is it not? In the wake of modernity, with its autonomic production of desires which gobble up and consume not only our sacred souls but also the very earth itself, are we not broken? Are we not spent? Are we not dazed, bewildered, and

---

5. Eliot, *Four Quartets*.

confused, and are we not desperately, rapaciously lonely? And is this not the case even for those of us who seek to transcend this condition through practices and rituals designed to calm and soothe our flagging spirits? Do we not hope desperately, and prematurely? Do we not love forcibly and possessively? Do we not trust, blindly, in whatever phantasm we have conjured up from the ruins of our creativity?

The one thing moderns do not do, ever, is pause, stop, empty ourselves, cease with that endless churning through of problems and solutions, all smoke and mirrors and digital shadows. We never command ourselves to be still in the nighttime of modernity—so that we may give ourselves over to unthinking, to unknowing, to a genuine hollowing out of every idea or ethic, whether good, bad, or indifferent. We do not call for an end to desire, which forever threatens to consume every object, or person, or effect of light or of landscape that wanders into our orbit. And this is true even in meditation as it is commonly practiced. For, as Slavoj Žižek rightly intuits, much of the consumer meditation industry is about patching up the tired and the stressed and the broken so that we can reengage in the very forms of neoliberal work, family, and entertainment that made us tired, stressed, and broken in the first place.[6]

What we need is a different form of life, a more deeply interfused weave of being, a more visceral form of relationship with each other and with the cosmos. What we need is to get outside of our neoliberal, differentiated selves. We need to get outside of the world we have created through the endless self-production of desire. What we need is to get out of our heads and our hearts in the direction of a radical openness to what the Indigenous nations of this continent call, quite simply, "country." Country is, for we natives, both radically material and radically divine. It is the embodiment of the divine in pathways, waterways, skyways, and the ritual songs that make them navigable. Country is, for us, a patterned network of reciprocal kinship with all living things: plants, animals, people, weather patterns, and even rocks, which vibrate with ancestral presence. Each of us are born to a specific country, and there we belong. Country tells us who we are, to whom we belong, and what our part will be in the profound responsibility to care for country and its strong but fragile ecologies. If we take our part in the communal vocation of caring for country, all of country will care for us.

Crucially, this sense of vocation is not something Indigenous people choose as the autonomous selves of neoliberal imagination might. It is,

6. Žižek, *On Belief*, 13–15.

rather, something that is simply *given* in the way things are, regardless of how we might perceive or respond to what is given. It is a vocation that is ours before we can choose, for country and the patterned moieties which give ethical substance to our responsibility simply precede and exceed the individual sense of self.[7] That does not mean, of course, that we cannot resist what is given. Indeed, insofar as we have been colonized along with everyone else, that possibility becomes ever more possible. But that is not what our calling is. And the further we move away from that call, the more unwell we become in body, mind, and spirit. For to resist the call of country is to accede to a consumerist agenda which has no mind or care for either country or the people whose job, for five thousand generations, has been the care of country. All consumerism cares about is the enrichment of the few through the exploitation of the many.

In Aboriginal perspective, then, as much as in the Christian mysticism of Mr. Eliot, the answer to our woes lies not within, but without: in country, or the givenness of things in themselves, rather than in what we would forge from them out of selves that look only to possess, to consume, and to colonize. To walk on country is not, therefore, simply to bathe oneself in the sensuality of occasional contact with the wonders of "nature"—wonderfully healing though this experience can be in itself—but also to stop and to stay, to engage in a more sustained waiting, to observe how each thread of the tapestry depends on each other thread for its life and its purpose. To wait long enough to see that life and death and life again are woven into the fabric of the bush, just as Christ and his paschal self-emptying are woven into the persistent creativity of the cosmos.

Which brings me, at the last, to the very next lines in Eliot's poem:

> Whisper of running streams, and winter lightning.
> The wild thyme unseen and the wild strawberry,
> The laughter in the garden, echoed ecstasy
> Not lost, but requiring, pointing to the agony
> > Of death and birth.

Let us, like country itself, be contemplatives who are willing to die to ourselves—to our hungry and self-serving desire for the phantasmic dreams of modernity—that we might be reborn to that more expansive self that is a deep and abiding kinship with all creation.

---

7. I am adapting, here, the philosophical theology of donation or givenness as proposed by Jean-Luc Marion in texts such as *In Excess* and *Prolegomena*.

CHAPTER 6

Decolonizing Scripture

THE NATIONAL ANTHEM, THE COLONIAL IMAGINATION, AND THE FICTION OF TERRA NULLIUS

For those fortunate enough to have never sung it before, here are the verses of the Australian national anthem as adopted by the Parliament of Australia in April 1984:

> Australians all let us rejoice,
> For we are young and free;
> We've golden soil and wealth for toil;
> Our home is girt by sea;
> Our land abounds in nature's gifts
> Of beauty rich and rare;
> In history's page, let every stage
> Advance Australia Fair.
> In joyful strains then let us sing,
> Advance Australia Fair.
>
> Beneath our radiant Southern Cross
> We'll toil with hearts and hands;
> To make this Commonwealth of ours
> Renowned of all the lands;
> For those who've come across the seas
> We've boundless plains to share;
> With courage let us all combine
> To Advance Australia Fair.
> In joyful strains then let us sing,
> Advance Australia Fair.

It is a song that I have never personally sung. On those occasions when, as part of a school or civic assembly, I was invited to sing the anthem, I declined. I still decline. Why? Because, as a trawloolway man whose family has lived in northern lutruwita/Tasmania for at least thirty-five thousand years, I will not sing the victory songs of the invader.

For, make no mistake, this is a victory song. It is an anthem that entrenches and encourages the myth of *terra nullius*, a British fantasy about this allegedly empty land that has now been legitimately occupied by free and hardworking pioneers who deserve the spoils of their adventuring on the underside of the globe.[1] The anthem is, in fact, a prominent example of the persistence of *terra nullius* in settler society. It functions to hide and obfuscate the truth of this nation's history, one that includes the stealing of these lands by absentee landlords from Britain; theft that was accomplished through the agency of paid servants from the working and criminal classes who waged bloody war against the Aboriginal and Torres Strait Islander nations who were already here; removal of survivors of these wars from our lands into camps where the speaking of our languages and the practice of our religions and cultures were usually outlawed; and forced indentured servitude and slavery both in these camps and on the newly stolen lands of white settlers. Despite some gains, most of us still do not have access to our own lands, sacred stories, or elders, and we remain amongst the most impoverished, unwell, and incarcerated people on the planet. Unfortunately, as historians such as Ann Curthoys and Meredith Lake have shown, it was also settler colonial readings of Bible stories about an "exodus" and the conquest of a "promised land" that contributed to the unfolding of these atrocities on Aboriginal country.[2]

That history is written on the landscape where I grew up in the "Kentish" region of northern lutruwita/Tasmania, where very few of the punilerpanna names for that place survive. Instead, you will today encounter a biblical landscape which features places like "Paradise," "Beulah," "Promised Land," and the "Gog Range." Here the conquerors sought to destroy and displace all trace of our people and replace it with the topography of the Bible lands.

---

1. Greg Lehman explores this mythology through the early art history of the colony of Van Diemen's Land, revealing that most colonial art pretended that Aboriginal people were either never here, or else were only here as either noble savages or wicked sub-humans who have now "disappeared." See his unpublished thesis, "Regarding the Savages."

2. Curthoys, "Expulsion"; Lake, *Bible*, 88–111.

In what follows, I will interrogate these stories of conquest as they appear in the biblical books of Deuteronomy and Joshua. But before that, I will say some things about how this same Bible might be read within an Aboriginal theology.

POSTFOUNDATIONALISM, OR HOW TO TAKE RESPONSIBILITY FOR OUR INTERPRETATIONS

I am not a biblical scholar, so my investigations of the Bible cannot possibly delve into the nitty-gritty of what the Bible allegedly says or doesn't say "in its own terms." I leave that to the biblical scholars who, in my personal experience, are far smarter than I could ever be. My task is more modest: to articulate a theology of Scripture which seeks to liberate the Bible from the colonial church and place it in the hands of Indigenous people. This is to declare, up front, three basic assumptions about Scripture which I happily own from the outset.

First, I take Scripture to be a collection of writings that were put together within Israel and within the early church at times of national or religious crisis, specifically the invasion of Israel and Judah by the Persian and Babylonian empires, respectively; and, later, in the case of the Christian writings, the advent of the Jesus movement within Judaism, and the destruction of Jerusalem by the Roman Empire. This is to place Scripture explicitly within a sociopolitical context of theological disputation about how people of faith ought to live within a colonized setting. The Scriptures, in other words, give us a snapshot in time of various arguments that were occurring between different schools of theology about who God is and about how the communities who belong to that God ought to respond to the encroachment into their lives of imperial overlords.[3]

A second assumption follows on from that. If the Scriptures offer snapshots of theological disputation, they cannot be read as seamlessly consistent in their messaging. The writings are irreducibly contextual, and are produced to critique, encourage, condemn, promote, and otherwise recommend highly idiosyncratic versions of how a faith community ought to live within the constrictions of empire. Much of Scripture seeks to interpret what is happening in the present by looking to remembered theological models from the past, models that were rarely written down but passed on

3. A helpful overview that takes this point of view is Howard-Brook, *"Come Out."* I'm grateful to Dean McDonald for drawing this text to my attention.

orally and ritually. Whenever such models are invoked, they are nevertheless tweaked, changed, and modified to address apparently new questions and challenges. This creates a pattern within Scripture of both faithfulness and unfaithfulness: the past is faithfully invoked, but most often in a way which, in fact, modifies the meaning of the past to make it more contextually alive to a present challenge. This process of creatively deconstructing older models and reconstructing them for a present challenge is, I would suggest, at the very heart of every theological enterprise based upon the way Scripture interprets itself. This enterprise can also be called preaching, for short.

A third assumption is connected to the creativity we have identified. If Scripture is indeed as I have described it, then the reading community must take full responsibility for the way in which Scripture is interpreted. That is, to openly confess and admit that when we say "Scripture says," what we really mean is "we believe (that is, hope and pray that) Scripture says." For whenever we take a point of view based upon some level of engagement with Scripture, what we are doing (whether we are aware of it or not) is reconstructing Scripture for our own, entirely idiosyncratic and contextual, purposes.[4] Which, as it turns out, is a deeply scriptural thing to do. Positively, this means that poor, colonized, and otherwise marginalized communities of faith can find in Scripture theological models and resources that powerfully and usefully address our struggles and conundrums. Negatively, it means that people of power and privilege can also interpret Scripture, very often in ways which baptize and bless their power and privilege. The point, here, is that Scripture can be made to say anything you want it to say. So let's be open and honest, please. Let's own the centrality of our own interests in the use we make of Scripture.

You may be asking, at this point, what does God want us to make of Scripture? Isn't the divine voice of primary importance in our reading of Scripture? Isn't the voice of God precisely what we are searching for as we read? Yes, absolutely. That fact is not at issue. I'd like you to notice, however, that our sense of the divine voice very often aligns, completely, with the way we read Scripture. If we believe that God is on the side of the oppressed,

---

4. I've been deeply influenced, in this regard, by Roland Barthes' essay "The Death of the Author" in which he argues that once a piece of writing is published, authorial intention is effectively "dead" or without stabilizing power, even if the author is still alive and readily identifiable. The reader, as the one who reconstructs the meaning of a text through the act of reading, takes over the meaning-making task from the author. The reader, in a sense, becomes a new author of the text. See Barthes, "Death."

we will privilege the biblical stories about a God who rescues slaves and becomes a slave Godself. If we believe that God wants us to live as nuclear families, we will privilege texts about household arrangements that are consistent with a male and female parent and their biological children. If we believe that God is love, we will take issue with texts that appear to condone genocide, matricide, and ecocide. If we believe that God hates gay people, then we are unlikely to give much credence to the story of the love between David and Jonathan. And so on. Very often, our views about the divine are formed in culture (ecclesial or otherwise), and we take those views to the text to have them confirmed or disconfirmed. Sometimes our views about God are formed by the reading of Scripture itself, and we take those impressions to culture and experience to have them confirmed or disconfirmed. Either way, Scripture cannot be said to be the last word on God. For God does not speak with one voice in Scripture. God appears to have at least as many voices as Scripture itself. This means that, if we are honest, we ought to take as much responsibility for our beliefs about the divine as we do for our interpretations of Scripture. When we say "God says," what we really mean is "we believe (that is, hope and pray that) God says."

The point of view I am spelling out here has been called "post-foundationalism,"[5] which is a fancy way of saying that when it comes to matters of theology and the interpretation of Scripture, no one has an insider track to the divine mind. No one has a God's-eye view. Each of us approach the divine as interpreters of a mystery which is far too intricately woven into the fabric of the universe for us to entirely comprehend. At best, we can give what is revealed our dedicated attention, and we can make educated guesses based upon what we see, hear, feel, touch, taste, and intuit of the divine presentation. We can also take full responsibility for our decisions to honor this version or that of the divine mystery, and live within that responsibility with conviction, consistency, and integrity.

Now, as you will have gathered from everything else I've written in this little book, I happen to believe in a divine reality which can be discerned in both country and Bible. I come to that conclusion because of the twin Aboriginal and Christian influences on me as I was growing up, both. But the decision to live into those influences, to immerse myself in those traditions of knowing and acting, is mine alone. I could have gone elsewhere. I could have become a Mahayana Buddhist, for example, or a scientific atheist. I could have jettisoned either my Aboriginal cosmology or my Christian

5. See, for example, Forster, "Post-Foundational."

Trinitarianism. But I didn't. Still I choose, each day I rise from my bed, to persevere with the gifts I was given in the tutelage of my family and the communion of being I discern in both country and church—most probably because I experience them as gifts, even if there's a small dose of poison in there as well. The "poison" has to do with the biblical fundamentalism of the Christian tradition in which I was raised, a fundamentalism that could conceive of no gap or distance between biblical voices and the divine voice; a fundamentalism that seemed, always and consistently, to be on the side of white settlers, especially their men. I chose, as a young man, to read the Bible in a way that was consistent with my trawloolway sensibilities, including a nascent longing for justice. That was hard work, in the beginning, because the settler community in which I was raised had no room for such thinking. But I have become stronger, over time, more at ease with my choices. And I have found other communities of reading with which to commune, most latterly an international community of Indigenous Christians who share many of my convictions.

"TEXTS OF TERROR"—BUT IT'S NOT ALL BAD

Scripture contains, in Phyliss Trible's memorable phrase, a great many "texts of terror."[6] Her own work concentrated on those parts of the biblical narratives that seemed especially horrible for women. Arguably, as a white woman of means, dear Phyllis missed a lot of the connections those texts had into the lived experience of women of "color." But her book was a groundbreaking piece of analysis for second-wave feminists. Indigenous readers have identified parts of the Bible that are equally as horrible for First Nations people. I'd like to identify and briefly comment on two of them now.

The first is a collection of texts that occur in Deuteronomy chapters 7 through 9. I select just one representative paragraph:

> When Yahweh your Elohim brings you into the land that you are
> about to enter and occupy, and he clears away many nations before
> you—the Hittites, the Girgashites, the Amorites, the Canaanites,
> the Perizzites, the Hivites, and the Jebusites, seven nations mighti-
> er and more numerous than you— and when Yahweh your Elohim
> gives them over to you and you defeat them, then you must utterly
> destroy them. Make no treaty with them and show them no mercy.

6. Trible, *Texts of Terror.*

> Do not intermarry with them, giving your daughters to their sons
> or taking their daughters for your sons, for that would turn away
> your children from following me, to serve other Elohims. Then the
> anger of Yahweh would be kindled against you, and he would de-
> stroy you quickly. But this is how you must deal with them: break
> down their altars, smash their pillars, hew down their sacred poles
> (Asherah), and burn their idols with fire. For you are a people holy
> to Yahweh your Elohim; Yahweh your Elohim has chosen you out
> of all the peoples on earth to be his people, his treasured posses-
> sion. (Deut 7:1–6, NRSV adapted)

To everyone whose primary picture of the divine is the Jesus of the gospels, this version of God might come as something of a surprise. Here God is called "Yahweh" and this God seems quite intent on genocide, that is, the complete destruction of the indigenous tribes of Canaan to make way for the people of Israel, whom he had chosen as his own. The book of Deuteronomy is a text that was authored during the forced exile of Judah's rulers and intellectuals to Babylon between 597 and 581 BCE. The authors place most of the book's content in the mouth of Moses, the renowned prophet and leader who led the Hebrew people from slavery in Egypt to the "promised land" of Canaan. The story of escape from slavery is obviously one that colonized peoples can work with. But not this. Not this sermon from the mouth of Moses, who addresses the people who are to enter the land of Canaan and declares that Yahweh would have them kill every single human being to possess it. To Indigenous ears, this sounds like a theological justification for genocide, and we know that many colonists invoked precisely these kinds of texts to justify their murder of our people and the wholesale destruction of our spiritual cultures.[7] A telling example is that of William Broughton, the first Anglican bishop of Australia, who paraphrased some of the language of Deuteronomy 7–9 in his 1830 report to the Colonial Office on why the Aboriginal people of Van Diemen's Land had resisted British invasion. Because of their "wanton and savage spirit," he said, because of their wickedness (cf. Deut 9:4, 5). And that report became an influential paradigm for the brutal treatment of Indigenous people in other parts of the Australian continent.[8]

What those who cite such passages to justify genocide fail to recognize is that these texts are theological propaganda, produced by an exilic school of theology seeking an answer to the questions, "Why has Yahweh

7. The classic essay in this regard is Warrior, "Native American."

8. Boyce, *God's Own Country*, 13–15.

sent us to exile in Babylon?" and "What sin have we committed to deserve this punishment?" The answer of the Deuteronomists was that Israel had failed to clear the land of its indigenous tribes, and thereafter intermarried with them and became worshippers of their evil gods and followers of their wicked ethical practices. What is lacking here is any sense of irony about the situation of the Deuteronomists, themselves, whose captors in Babylon not only allowed them to live, but also to practice and celebrate their culture and religion. Eventually they were allowed to return to Jerusalem and rebuild both the city and its temple to Yahweh.

Why could the Deuteronomists not see that keeping people alive, and entering some kind of mutually beneficial treaty with the people of the land, is a worthy model? Probably because they were proto-puritans who could never come to terms with the real-world need for compromise and treaty. A negotiated outcome was certainly the preferred model for some of the other theological schools in the exile, as we shall see with the Abraham cycle of stories in chapter 8. But there are other alternatives in Scripture as well. The story of Esther, for all its difficulties in the eyes of feminists, nevertheless tells a story in which marrying someone from another religion and culture can become a means of *saving* your people from death and guaranteeing their flourishing. Add to that the perspective of some of the exilic and postexilic prophets, who imagined a people of God gathered not from one chosen people, but from many.

A second set of terror-producing texts are those found in the margins of Joshua and Judges concerning the way in which survivors of the attempted genocide were to be treated. For example,

> "Because it was told to your servants for a certainty that Yahweh your Elohim had commanded his servant Moses to give you all the land, and to destroy all the inhabitants of the land before you; so we were in great fear for our lives because of you, and did this thing. And now we are in your hand: do as it seems good and right in your sight to do to us." This is what he did for them: he saved them from the Israelites; and they did not kill them. But on that day Joshua made them hewers of wood and drawers of water for the congregation and for the altar of Yahweh, to continue to this day, in the place that he should choose. (Josh 9:24–27 NRSV adapted)

Here is another Deuteronomic text, this time concerning the fate of the Gibeonites, another indigenous tribe in the land promised to Israel.

According to the book of Joshua, the Gibeonites were a cunning people who found a way to trick the invading Hebrews into making treaty with them. Having roughed up their appearance and their goods to produce the impression that they had come to the promised land from somewhere far away, they sought a treaty with Joshua which was granted because Joshua believed their story. Of course, the truth of the Gibeonites' indigeneity comes out very soon thereafter. But, having made a treaty for the preservation of their lives, Joshua chooses to enslave the Gibeonites rather than kill them. From that time until "this day" the Gibeonites had lived amongst the Israelites as indentured laborers: slaves.

This elaborate story accomplishes two things for Deuteronomistic theology. It explains why so many treaties were made with indigenous tribes that the Hebrew people had been commanded to kill. But it also explains the presence of slaves in Israel, slaves apparently taken from the indigenous population. As you make your way through the books of Joshua and Judges, you will find multiple references to both the survival of Canaanite tribes, but also to their enslavement (cf. Josh 13:13; 15:63; 16:10; 17:12). The phrase, "they live amongst the people to this day as hewers of wood and carriers of water" functions as a theological shorthand for this fact.

There is bad news and good news in these texts for Aboriginal and Torres Strait Islander peoples. The bad news is that these texts can, and have, been used to justify the practice of enslavement. The historical record shows that children who were removed from their families and placed in orphanages became unpaid domestic servants of either the mission authorities or the private white households in which they were then placed.[9] Similarly, many Aboriginal people became the property of station owners when their land was sold out from underneath them. People worked for food. Women and young boys could be used as the sexual playthings of station managers. Rebelling against management could get them killed.[10]

The good news in these texts is that even genocidal puritans like the Deuteronomists had to recognize that treaties were, in fact, forged and indigenous tribes survived. Indeed, many of these people may have been part of the clans that eventually became the federation named Israel from the very beginning. This may not have been their preferred history. But it happened nevertheless, and even the Deuteronomists had to come to terms

9. Haskins, "Sickness."

10. The classic study is Berndt and Berndt, *End of an Era*. See also Anthony, "Criminal Justice."

with the fact. As a nation dominated by settler colonists, Australia is still ill at ease with the fact that Aboriginal and Torres Strait Islander people have survived the genocidal policies of the crown. We are here. Many of us are even beginning to overcome the intergenerational trauma and poverty that is ours as a colonized people. Some of us are thriving! Not that our survival is a truth that settlers are entirely prepared for. They continue to spout old myths about our peoples "dying out" because of the effects of disease upon our inferior genetic material; or about the peaceful settlement of these "empty" lands by hardworking pioneers; or about the goodness of the missionaries who protected us from criminals and taught us the virtues of European civilization and religion. We continue to be lectured, in some circles, about how "lucky" we were to be colonized by the British, because "the Spanish and the Portuguese were far worse." Our survival means that settlers are forced to reckon with a different version of their history, a version told from the vantage point of mob on "the other side of the frontier,"[11] and the experience is indeed quite painful for many.

Christian settlers, in particular, are starting to see that there are direct connections between the story of Israel's occupation of their "promised land" and the invasion of Australia, with all its many consequences for mob. Some are facing that history, however painful. Many are not. But there is still time. Perhaps it will be the young who will own this history in a way in which their elders cannot. Perhaps their exposure to revised history curriculums in school will make a difference. Perhaps the visible presence of Indigenous people in sporting codes, in Parliament, in business and at work, at university and at theological colleges will make a difference. We have learned, through bitter experience, not to hope for too much. And yet, I smell the winds of change.

A MORE INDIGENOUS BIBLICAL PARADIGM: COMMUNING WITH THE DIVINE IN THE SONG OF SONGS[12]

As regularly as I can, I venture into lonely forest walks around the coastal settlement of Bridport in northeast Tasmania. Whilst I have no illusions about the flora and fauna bearing much relation to that of a time prior to

---

11. A phrase taken from Henry Reynolds in his book of the same name: Reynolds, *Other Side.*

12. This section began as a paper given at a symposium celebrating the launch of Mark Brett's book on December 12, 2019. See Brett, *Locations of God.*

European annexation, I nevertheless take great comfort in walking there, in following the contoured rise and fall of land and sea and communing with my pairebeenener ancestors as I do so.

I use the word "commune" deliberately. For that is what happens when I walk. Something of myself flows into the ancestral aliveness of land and sea; the ancestral community—she or he or they—are changed by my presence, the specificity of my body in space and time, my odor and breath, my breathing, and the soundings I make by sensual contact and by vocalization. And something of that aliveness flows into whomever I am, also. The shape and form of sea and land as he leads me toward secret grottos and streams; her breathy, salty atmosphere caressing eye and ear and skin; the sounds made by wind and sea as they flow around ancient trees and rockscapes; the thud and thump of furry kin as they pad their way, unseen, across the forest floor: a sign and a promise of an occasional more fulsome encounter, face-to-face. By this communion, this asymmetrical exchange of greater and lesser selves, we are both changed. The ancestral landscape is enlarged to account for and address myself, my presence, my unique *haecceitas*. And I, myself, become "all flame," as Abba Joseph would have it,[13] an instance in one time and place of the ancestral fire who inhabits and animates all times and places; a moment of rejoicing in which the ancestral song becomes a single singer; an instance, a momentary fluctuation, by which the ancestral ocean becomes a single ebb or flow of tidal movement. In this communion I find, momentarily at least, some kind of healing, an ointment to soothe and to seal all the scars that I carry, in body and in mind. But the healing is far from complete. It is incremental and partial. It is real, it is effective; but it is unmasterable. It gives itself certainly, but only as a gift; it will not obey any law of necessity, annexation, or measured exchange I might try to impose from the colonial imagination.

The ancestor I commune with has a name but cannot be fully and finally named with this name. The name I know, the name that has survived, is moinee. Moinee is the creator ancestor most widely invoked and revered by my people. She is the wombat ancestor who initiated the formation of the land of lutruwita or Tasmania which, of course, is alive with the presence of many other ancestors as well. Amongst the lesser ancestors is parlevar the kangaroo, the totem of my particular clan, the one on whom the first palawa or human beings were modelled, albeit with significant modifications. Both moinee and parlevar still appear to us in their animal forms:

13. Desert Fathers, *Sayings*, 103.

they are concretely and unmistakably there whenever we stand face-to-face with our sister wombat or brother kangaroo. And the times when I have done so over the years, the moments in which some kind of inarticulate conversation can be said to have taken place, are truly the most joyful and the most holy of my life. So, I know with whom I commune. And yet I do not know.

For really it is clear that the wombat and the kangaroo, for all their magnificence, are a lot like you or I: unique moments, instances, expressions or substitutes who are what they are because some greater life or power animates them and puts them in play. That life or power can clearly be named or even gendered in particular instances. Likewise, it can be communed with through the mediation of particular forms or material events in country, air or seascape. But can the "Thou" with whom we commune be named as she or he or they are, in his or her or their own being? Can she be named, as it were, comprehensively, without remainder or doubt, in her time beyond a particular time and her place beyond a particular place? Can he be named, as Jean-Luc Marion would have it, in her divinity beyond being?[14] Not really. For every name is, as Jacques Derrida has taught us, a trace or cipher for an identity that is, in the fullness of its self-revelation, neither fully here nor fully now. "Now we see in part and we know in part," said St. Paul, "as in a mirror, dimly" (1 Cor 13:9, 12). The time for knowing the divine identity, as we are fully known by the divine, has not yet arrived. We do not even know who Christ is, or we ourselves in Christ, not completely. Not comprehensively. What we do know is that the name we do know evokes in us a desire or a longing to know more fully.

The themes I've developed through my reading of ancestral country may also be found in the Hebrew Bible's *Song of Songs*. If, that is, you have the ears to hear. After all, the divine is never comprehensively named in the poem, not even as Yahweh, that most common of names for God in the Hebrew canon. Yet, if it is read within its canonical religious context and the history of its reception by both Jews and Christians, this poem about the longing of the black-skinned "Shulamite" for her lover may also be read as a celebration of the communion between human beings and the divine as it is mediated by the particularity of landscape or country.[15]

14. Marion, *God without Being*.

15. For an entirely Aboriginal perspective on country as the sacred feminine, please consult Evans, "Giving Voice."

Let's first talk about landscape or country. The poem is full of phrases which describe the lovers' bodies as features of a cultivated landscape or else as the fauna that inhabits that landscape. Here are some examples:

> My beloved is to me a cluster of henna blossoms in the vineyards of En-gedi. (Song 1:14)

> As an apple tree amongst the trees of the wood, so is my beloved among young men. With great delight I sat in his shadow and his fruit was sweet to my taste (Song 2:3)

> Arise my love, my fair one, and come away; for now the winter is past and the rain is over and gone. The flowers appear on the earth; the time of singing has come, and the voice of the turtledove is heard in our land. The fig tree puts forth its figs and the vines are in blossom; they give forth fragrance. Arise my love, my fair one, and come away. O my dove, in the clefts of the rock, in the covert of the cliff, let me see your face, let me hear your voice; for your voice is sweet and your face is lovely (Song 2:10–14)

> How beautiful you are my love, how very beautiful! Your eyes are doves behind your veil. Your hair is like a flock of goats, moving down the slopes of Gilead . . . Your cheeks are like halves of a pomegranate behind your veil . . . Your two breasts are like two fawns, twins of a gazelle, that feed among the lilies. (Song 4:1, 3b, 5)

In my view, the landscape imagery of the poem is very often so dense and entangled that it is difficult for the reader to determine what image is standing in for what reality. Are the lover's breasts, for example, the reality for which twin fawns are a signifier, or is the reality the gazelles and the lover's breasts their signifier? Paul Ricouer, for his part, has argued that the intensity of these metaphors has the effect of dissociating the metaphorical network from its support in any specific human history.[16] This means that the various characters or voices in the poem come to stand in for one another in so echolalic a manner that it is often difficult to discern who is lover and who is beloved and who, indeed, are the friends who apparently discuss their love. Furthermore, as we have seen, the landscape itself often seems to speak, to find agency.

The poem is, in fact, laden to the brim with such instances of indeterminism. Here are some examples. First, pieces of dialogue often appear to include quotations from someone other than the one who is speaking,

---

16. Ricoeur, "Nuptial Metaphor," 273–74.

with the result that it is difficult to identify the speaker (1:4b; 1:8; 2:1; 6:10). Second, there are several dream sequences that present a similar problem. Is the shepherd dreaming of being a king (3:6–11)? Is the Shulamite dreaming of being a peasant woman (5:2–8), or is it the other way around? Or are all these figures quite distinct from one another in the body? Third, there are evocations of memory that intertwine with the present in such a way that it is difficult to tell which is present and which is memory. The mother figure returns again and again in 1:6, 3:4, 3:11, 6:9, 8:1, and 8:4, but whose mother is she? Or is she the beloved as a younger woman? Finally, the seven "scenes" often referred to by commentators are said to begin with lover or beloved searching for each other, and to end with a consummation when they find each other. But these alleged "consummations" are very difficult to find, in fact, because they are sung with a sense of longing rather than recounted with any sense of material gravity or traction. These features suggest that the Song is not a narrative in which characters can be readily distinguished one from another, but a poem that explores the formation of a communion, a coinherence, of voice. The poem often asks the question "Who?" but the question is never entirely answered.

The reception history of the Song would seem to support this view. From the very beginning, the poem has been read as a sensual allegory of divine-human love. That this is so might appear to be something of an oddity when one considers that Judaism, Christianity, and Islam alone, amongst all the ancient religious traditions, appear to have no sacred rites of a sexually explicit nature. Julia Kristeva explains this by reference to an analogy with the biblical canon. The Song imagines the desire of God as a desire without consummation. There is no lovemaking at the maternal hearth in this erotic poem. Therefore, the Song, as with the canon as a whole, imagines the divine as one who loves, and is desired by human beings, but who remains allusive in some eschatological sense. Desire is not finally consummated, and so remains desire.[17]

Following Origen, who said that it is the "movements of love" in the *Song* which are more important than the identity of its characters, Ricoeur argues for an interpretation of the Song in which the "nuptial" metaphor for the relations between the lovers is "liberated" from a purely human reference. The Greek paradigm of erotic love tended to see the point of sexual entanglement as a means of ecstatic escape from the body into some kind of selfless and unconscious communion with the divine One. But that is

17. Kristeva, *Tales of Love*, 15.

not what is happening in the Song. Here the profound play of desire in the possession and dispossession of selves suggests, instead, a view of love that is transcendent and yet powerfully incarnational at the same time. What happens here is not a doing away with the sexual reference but rather its putting on hold or suspension; this then effects a freeing of the whole metaphorical network of nuptiality for other embodied "investments and divestments."[18] That possibility is further enhanced by the radical mobility of identification between the partners of the amorous dialogue and the landscapes in which they play, a mobility that smacks of the "substitution" of one ancestral instance or character for another, as I propose above in my reading of country.

On this basis, Kristeva argues that the lover in the Song can be legitimately interpreted as the cipher for an absent or incorporeal God who is nevertheless made available to the human beloved in ritual, as well as in the very ordinary landscape of human life. Supreme authority, whether it be royal or divine, can be loved as flesh while remaining essentially inaccessible; the intensity of love comes precisely from "that combination of received jouissance and taboo, from a basic separation that nevertheless unites."[19] This reminds me of parlevar, who most often promises an encounter with traces and sounds, igniting my longing, but who rarely appears to gaze at my face.

To these European insights I would add, of course, that all this sensual and eschatological charge is ignited in landscape, in sky, and in waterway; and that it is precisely because human selves come from ancestral country and are instances of the ancestral embedded in country that we are most ourselves as human beings when we commune with the divine by communing with country. Country is like the Christian God, in that it cannot be possessed or domesticated, used or even finally and comprehensively named. Country is like the Christ of God, whose life is poured out for us and for our salvation only insofar as we can respect and treasure the gift, and take it into ourselves, into our hearts and bodies, and love it with all the power that country so generously provides.

I suppose this means that I belong, also, to the school of Job as Mark Brett has described it in his *Locations of God*. Brett understands Job as a more fluid and poetic version of the exilic "priestly" school of theology, which wants to locate God not simply in the cry for a human form of justice

18. Ricoeur, "Nuptial Metaphor," 273–74.

19. Kristeva, *Tales of Love*, 90.

or liberation in the face of empire, but also in the wise utterances of creation itself, [20] in which God speaks particular words of wisdom for particular places.[21] This would certainly sit well with my peculiarly Aboriginal sense of responsibility for country: we cannot care for a particular place unless we first listen to what it is telling us—including that sense in which it would seek to love us—in its own unique voice. The particularity of that voice is for that country, and especially its caretakers, those who are related to that country as kin, as ancestral stewards. To listen, of course, is the very opposite of colonization and its bullyboy shouting. For the sake of us all, I pray we shall learn, in a timely manner, to listen more deeply to what our lands and seas and waterways are telling us.

20. Brett, *Locations*, 127.
21. Brett, *Locations*, 130.

CHAPTER 7

Enemies, Real and Imagined[1]

BIBLICAL REFLECTIONS ON THE FIGURE OF THE ENEMY

Enemies. We all have them. And, if we don't have any real enemies, we make them up. Or else we paint them in more dramatic terms than is strictly necessary. Observe, for example, what is happening in Ukraine at present. One of the key reasons Putin has publicly offered for invading Ukraine is that Ukraine's national leadership has been taken over by fascists, even "Nazis," who are oppressing the people. Now, from the point of view of the Ukrainians themselves, this seems extremely fanciful. But from the point of view of Putin, who has in mind the restoration of a past, mythical, Orthodox, Russian empire, the Ukrainian leadership are indeed the evil nazis who are keeping their people from participating in the glorious restoration.[2]

We need to be careful whom we call an enemy. Perhaps we should not call anyone an enemy, even if they explicitly choose that path and designation, for themselves. "Love your enemy," said Jesus in his famous sermon, "do good to those who hate you, bless those who curse you, and pray for those who abuse you" (Lk 6:27, 28). This is a tough teaching. If your neighbor is your enemy, what then? If you are the Karen or Chin villager whose house is being raided by the Myanmar military, what should you do? If you are an Aboriginal woman who has been raped by a British soldier, and your children killed before your eyes, how should you respond?

---

1. This chapter began life as a homily offered at Koonung Uniting Church in Lent 2022. Deverell, "Homily."

2. See Gotev, "Putin's Words."

Genesis 15 tells a story about the covenant or treaty Yahweh makes with Abram to preserve his progeny's legacy against every threat, real or imagined.

> After these things the word of the Lord came to Abram in a vision, "Do not be afraid, Abram, I am your shield; your reward shall be very great." But Abram said, "O Lord God, what will you give me, for I continue childless, and the heir of my house is Eliezer of Damascus?" And Abram said, "You have given me no offspring, and so a slave born in my house is to be my heir." But the word of the Lord came to him, "This man shall not be your heir; no one but your very own issue shall be your heir." He brought him outside and said, "Look towards heaven and count the stars, if you are able to count them." Then he said to him, "So shall your descendants be." And he believed the Lord; and the Lord reckoned it to him as righteousness . . .
>
> On that day the Lord made a covenant with Abram, saying, "To your descendants I give this land, from the river of Egypt to the great river, the river Euphrates, the land of the Kenites, the Kenizzites, the Kadmonites, the Hittites, the Perizzites, the Rephaim, the Amorites, the Canaanites, the Girgashites, and the Jebusites (Gen 15:1–6, 18–21).

If Abram is prepared to trust his future, and the future of his descendants to Yahweh, then Yahweh will make them as numerous "as the stars in the heaven" and the very land on which Abram stands, stretching from Egypt to the Euphrates, will belong to them. (Apparently, as we shall see, the current owners of the land in question are to be displaced.) Now, if you read this passage in its context, there are probably both legitimate and illegitimate grounds for Abram's anxiety. On the one hand, since arriving in Canaan, Abram had been caught up in a regional conflict between various city-states in which his nephew Lot was taken into captivity (14:8–16). He also, to this point, had not produced a legitimate heir, only a slave, the issue of a concubine (15:2).[3] On the other hand, Abram was an acquisitive man who was clearly deeply anxious about both his personal safety and wealth. The story about Abram selling his wife Sarai to Pharoah as a concubine, in exchange for sheep, cattle, donkeys and female slaves—primarily out of

---

3. This verse is probably best translated "O Lord God, what can you give me seeing that I shall die accursed, and the steward of my household is Dam-Mesek Elieze." In Hebrew, "Dam-Mesek" probably means "offspring of Mesek." The Septuagint reads: "Lord, what will You give me, seeing I go childless, and the heir of my house is Eliezer of Damascus, the son of Mesek, my domestic maid servant."

a concern that he will lose his own life—is as horrific a tale of patriarchal paranoia as you will find anywhere (12:10–20).

With this background in mind, perhaps we must conclude that whilst the treaty between Abram and Yahweh comes about at Yahweh's initiative, Abram's paranoia about the preservation of his socioeconomic legacy plays its part as well. An earlier version of the treaty (12:1–3) promises that Abram's descendants will become a blessing to all nations. Not their conquerors, but a source for their blessing. Perhaps that is what the covenant is supposed to be about. But this later version, in Genesis 15, seems more concerned with the ways in which the indigenous nations, the people already there in the land, are to be displaced by Abram's progeny and therefore seen as enemies, a threat to Abram's possessive ambitions (15:7–8, 18–21). This is an ambiguity that has been played out in that region from the time of the Hebrew patriarchs right through to the current conflicts between Arab and Jew in Israel/Palestine. And, of course, there were echoes of these fears and anxieties at play in the colonization of Australia where Aboriginal and Torres Strait Islander people were cast as the enemy because they stood in the way of an entirely legitimate occupation of these lands by white people.[4]

The face of an enemy appears quite regularly in the Psalms as well. In Psalm 27, for example, the poet describes his fear of an enemy that has surrounded him on every side and wants to take his life.

> When evildoers assail me
>   to devour my flesh—
> my adversaries and foes—
>   they shall stumble and fall.
> Though an army encamp against me,
>   my heart shall not fear;
> though war rise up against me,
>   yet I will be confident.
>
> Now my head is lifted up
>   above my enemies all around me,
> and I will offer in his tent
>   sacrifices with shouts of joy;
> I will sing and make melody to the Lord.

4. See Curthoys, "Expulsion," for a rich exploration of the ways in which biblical narratives shaped the colonial imagination.

Teach me your way, O Lord,
    and lead me on a level path
    because of my enemies.

Do not give me up to the will of my adversaries,
    for false witnesses have risen against me,
    and they are breathing out violence. (Ps 27:2, 3, 6, 11, 12)

The poem is an appeal to the Lord for refuge and help against that enemy. Most white suburban Bible study groups I know usually read these psalms as if they, themselves, are the Psalmist and someone else is the enemy. But what if that isn't the case? Have you ever tried to read a psalm, or any other biblical passage, as if you weren't the victim/hero in the story? Have you ever considered the ways in which you, yourselves, might be the enemy? An enemy of the earth and of its flora and fauna, for example, or an enemy of the indentured classes of labor who make our clothes? Or an enemy of Indigenous people, because you stole our lands and continue to benefit from our dispossession and hardship? How would that make a difference to your reading of sacred Scripture? Erna Kim Hackett says:

> . . . white Christianity suffers from a bad case of Disney princess theology. As each individual reads Scripture, they see themselves as the princess in every story. They are Esther, never Xerxes or Haman. They are Peter, but never Judas. They are the woman anointing Jesus, never the Pharisees. They are the Jews escaping slavery, never Egypt. For citizens of the most powerful country in the world, who enslaved both Native and Black people, to see itself as Israel and not Egypt when studying Scripture is a perfect example of Disney princess theology. And it means that as people in power, they have no lens for locating themselves rightly in Scripture or society—and it has made them blind and utterly ill-equipped to engage issues of power and injustice.[5]

Hackett is a Native American who is commenting upon the situation in the United States. But her observation is surely apt for the settler-dominant churches in Australia as well.

If we turn to Pauline tradition, the writer to the Philippians says that the enemy is not so much opposed to particular people, or even to Christ, but rather to the cross of Christ.

> Brothers and sisters, join in imitating me, and observe those who live according to the example you have in us. For many live as

5. Hackett, "Why."

enemies of the cross of Christ; I have often told you of them, and now I tell you even with tears. Their end is destruction; their god is the belly; and their glory is in their shame; their minds are set on earthly things. But our citizenship is in heaven, and it is from there that we are expecting a Saviour, the Lord Jesus Christ. He will transform the body of our humiliation so that it may be conformed to the body of his glory, by the power that also enables him to make all things subject to himself. (Phil 3:17–21)

Here the enemy is written not as someone who wants to steal your possessions or kill you, but rather as one who is allergic to suffering in the cause of justice. For these kinds of enemy worship another god, "their stomach," an ancient way of speaking about the sin of gluttony or personal acquisitiveness, the sin of accumulating all things to yourself at the expense of many others. There is a sense, here, in which Philippians might be read as a critique of the acquisitive nature of Abram in Genesis 15—Abram could be understood as the "enemy," for he seems concerned only about his legacy, the land he steals from others, and the prosperity of his own family and clan. The writer to the Philippians prefers a citizenship that is not so self-absorbed but participates, instead, in the sufferings of Christ for the sake of a commonwealth that is "in heaven," that is, in a place and a time that has yet to arrive. In that "heaven" which, in my Aboriginal reframing of New Testament eschatology, is a figure for the sovereignty of country, the ancestor Christ works to transform the humiliated bodies of all who have suffered injustice and degradation and marginalization, into the form of his own glorious body, which is at one with the primordial dreaming. In other words, all that is wrong and unfair can be put right. All that is broken can be restored. This is good news for all who suffer, or who are broken and marginalized. But it doesn't happen by magic. You must live out of the gift that has already been given.

Finally, in Luke's Gospel, it is instructive to learn about the enemy from Jesus, whose most immediate foe is Herod, the puppet king of the Roman occupation. Herod is obviously so afraid of Christ's teaching that he has put out a "hit" on him (13:31). Christ's response to this news is quite extraordinary. Rather than go into hiding, rather than gathering a militia to protect himself, what Christ does is offer a lament over Jerusalem, a city divided against itself, a city that will at once listen to a prophet's preaching and honor a prophet's office, but also, in time, kill that prophet for speaking inconvenient or uncomfortable words (13:34–35). Jesus himself, as indicated in the final verses of this passage, will himself be welcomed by the

Jerusalemites as a prophet and even a messiah but, within the week, be killed by those same Jerusalemites. Here the enemy is within. Not the other, someone from another group or tribe, ethnicity, or religion. The enemy is your friend, your comrade, your congregation, your synagogue, your church, your ethnic group. The enemy is those closest to you and about whom you care the most. In the face of enemies such as these, Christ teaches us to lament, which is an ancient way of naming the evil and injustice of which we are capable; but also to persevere in opposition to the enemy's preferred outcomes. The words of Jesus when he hears of Herod's plans are instructive:

> Go tell that fox, "I will go on driving out demons and healing people today and tomorrow and, on the third day reach my goal."
> In any case, I must press on today and tomorrow and the next day, for surely no prophet can die outside of Jerusalem. (Lk 13:32, 33)

Here there is no hint of revenge or strategizing towards getting the upper hand. There is a simple acceptance of the awful truth of the situation and a deep-down determination to stand firm in the fight against evil, no matter what the likely outcome.

There is much to learn, here, for those of us who have suffered the consequences of invasion and the annexation of our sovereign lands. I long ago abandoned all hope that we, as Aboriginal and Torres Strait Islander nations, could ever dig ourselves out of the hole we find ourselves in. We are too busy imitating the colonizer by fighting with each other to present a united front.

Certainly, there is little political will towards justice from the colonizer, at least insofar as the political class can be said to represent the will of the people. Colonizers, and particularly the mining, forestry, and agricultural companies that continue to enjoy extraordinary levels of subsidized support from the taxpayer, benefit enormously from our dispossession and marginalization. And they continue to destroy, wound, and maim country to make their profits. In my estimation, we have little to look forward to from these sectors but an endless attitude of charitable paternalism, breadcrumbs from the imperial table.

What can the person of faith do, then, except to be as honest and as truthful as one can be, to name what is really the case in the presence of the colonizing powers, to lament that it is so, and to fight the good fight? In this there is a faith, against all the trends of the age, that our bodies of humiliation can be transformed into bodies of glory. How that might come to be remains, for me at least, a profound and quite impenetrable mystery. But without the cosmic overlay that Christians called "resurrection faith" and Aboriginal people call the resilience of country for life through death, there is nothing to look forward to at all. The enemy, after all, is a version of death that would stand alone in its finality, as the very last word. But we Aboriginal people are wedded to the conviction that country is for us, not against us, and that, when we die, we return to country and contribute to her ongoing capacity to create life from the compost of death. There are resonances here with the Christian faith in the resurrection of the body, yet without the need for mythologizing a personal Jesus or the individualized resurrection of particular human persons.

ON THE LEGITIMACY OF DEFENDING ONESELF AND ONE'S COUNTRY

The war in Ukraine is, of course, just one of the conflicts raging in the world right now. For the moment, the conflicts in Palestine, Yemen, Syria, Ethiopia, Myanmar, and many other places, no longer enjoy sustained attention from international media organizations. The extent to which the following comments about the war in Ukraine might pertain, also, to these many other conflicts, I will leave to the reader to decide. I am no expert on the geopolitics of any of these places.

I begin by pointing out that, in this world at least, we are dealing not with the ultimate and the perfect but with the penultimate and the imperfect. So, whilst a more robust form of pacifism might suffice in the face of lesser forms of violence—refusing to fight in a morally ambiguous war in another part of the world, for example—pacifism of this kind does not seem sufficient when one's own land, livelihood, and the lives of one's loved ones are under threat. In the face of such clear and present danger, I believe the Christian has not merely a right, but a duty and responsibility, to mount some kind of defence.

My reasoning goes something like this. All life is sacred because it is brought into existence by the action of the creator. Inherent in the gift of life is a right and responsibility to maintain the conditions by which that life, within reasonable limits, can flourish and become what it was created to be. Insofar as that is possible without, simultaneously, seriously curtailing the flourishing of other forms of life, we might speak in this context of a "responsibility" to live and flourish. That word "responsibility" suggests that a life is lived before the one who gives it. That "one," I would posit—as both a Christian and trawloolway man—is the creator, the one who gives us life in all its myriad forms. We are responsible to our creator, however identified in various religious and spiritual traditions. We live our lives in a way which responds appropriately to what is given.

Now, human beings must take life for the sake of our sustenance and our thriving. We may take from what is given in creation, its flora and its fauna, to sustain our lives. But there are limits to what we may take. We may not, for example, hunt particular animals to the point where their own capacity to thrive and flourish is severely diminished. Neither may we do so with plant life. For if we do so, we risk compromising the entire biosphere's responsibility and capacity to flourish before, and to the glory of, our creator.

The same principle applies when it comes to human life, but perhaps in an even more robust form. Both the Jewish and Christian traditions put severe limits upon the taking of human life. "Thou shalt not kill," whilst not an absolute command which applies in any and all circumstances, nevertheless inscribes a serious duty to do everything possible to avoid the taking of human life.

What this means, I think, when it comes to the theater of war between human nations, is simply this: that one should avoid policies and practices that are likely to lead to war. One should never be the aggressor or the provocateur. One should never be the one who creates the conditions—whether these be political, cultural, economic, or environmental—in which war becomes the most likely outcome. We should do everything we can to avoid starting wars. For wars destroy life—not only human life, but also animal and plant life—on a scale which makes the likelihood of recovery exponentially difficult.

There are circumstances, however, in which war becomes inevitable. Having done all that is rationally and morally possible to avoid conflict with an aggressor, sometimes one simply must take up arms to defend one's right and responsibility to live and to flourish before the creator is a way that is commensurate with an equitable distribution of that right and responsibility across the whole biosphere.

An example, from the recent history of my own people, is the way we took up weapons to defend our country and our way of life from the British invasion, which took place in ever more disruptive and devastating waves from 1801 until the present. In the face of that invasion, which proceeded on the assumption that Aboriginal people enjoyed no right or responsibility to life and its flourishing, we had no choice. Before our creator ancestors, and because of their injunction to care for country and for each other, we had to fight. Now, the fact that we lost those wars and continue to sue for a more just settlement for our people and our country, means that the continent named "Australia" by the invader is no longer the ecological wonderland it once was. Thousands of species are now extinct because of the destruction of habitat. The ecological systems on which all of life depends are now either dead or dying in much of the continent. And the right and responsibility of Aboriginal peoples to life and flourishing—precisely as we care for country—remains of little consequence to our religious, commercial, or political leaders.

But we had to fight. To preserve the way of life to which our creator ancestors had called us. To prevent the destruction of that way of life by a people who had little regard for the call and injunction of the creator. We lost, obviously. But we had to fight.

To the extent that the war in Ukraine mirrors what we have experienced ourselves, I would argue that the people of the Ukraine also have to fight. Before God, they must fight. For the sake of the way and form of human flourishing which God has given, they must fight. For the sake of resisting an evil and destructive ideology, they must fight. And we who believe in the sacredness of all forms of life, precisely as they are given in creation, must offer whatever forms of solidarity we can.

CHAPTER 8

Acknowledging Country[1]

Some of the discussions I've had with settlers of late have revealed that uttering an "acknowledgment of country" that communicates both respect and empathy is still just a little too tricky for many. Indeed, some are deeply unsure about what acknowledging country is all about. Here, in this very practical chapter, I've gathered the bits and pieces of guidance I've handed out over the past few years into a list of dos and don'ts. I've also attempted, towards the end, to articulate something of the theological vision that informs a respectful acknowledgment of country. I hope it is helpful. But let's begin with some bigger-picture definitions.

WHAT IS "COUNTRY" FOR ABORIGINAL AND TORRES STRAIT ISLANDER PEOPLE?

As discussed in previous chapters, "country" encompasses the lands, seas, waterways, and skyscapes of this continent. The First Peoples of this continent may be grouped into over three hundred nations, each having a sovereign and unceded responsibility to care for a particular part of the continent. Naarm (Melbourne), for example, belongs to the Kulin nations known as the Wurundjeri Woi-Wurrung and the Bunurong.[2] It is their

1. This chapter incorporates some paragraphs I wrote with Naomi Wolfe for the University of Divinity. See Deverell and Wolfe, "Protocol."

2. Note that colonization has left us with multiple English spellings for different nations and clans. Bunurong, for example, can also be rendered "Bunorong" or "Bun Wurrung." Similarly, trawloolway, my own nation, can be rendered "trawlwoolway" or

responsibility to care for the lands, seas, and waterways of Naarm and to ensure (insofar as it is possible in a colonized country) that any who live or visit there will respect the lore and traditions of the creator ancestors who made, and continue to inhabit, this country.

WHAT IS A "WELCOME TO COUNTRY"?

Before the arrival of colonists, strict protocols governed expeditions or visits into the country of another nation or clan. Upon approaching the borderlands, permission to enter that country had to be obtained from its elders. One had to make the purpose of the visit clear and agree to carefully abide by the lore of that country for as long as the visit lasted. Once an agreement had been negotiated, the visitors would be welcomed to that country by participating in a ritual which rendered those privileges and responsibilities real and active. On Kulin country this was known as the ceremony of "Tanderrum." Modern "welcome to country" ceremonies are derived from these more ancient practices but are now offered in a decidedly colonial context where the capacity of elders to care for their country is greatly diminished because of unresolved issues around access, ownership, and the capacity to keep knowledge systems alive.

A modern welcome to country ceremony must be presided over by an elder or authorized representative of the clan or nation on whose country the ceremony is to be held. In Naarm, for example, this must be an elder or authorized representative of the Wurundjeri or Bunurong. In tarntanya/ Adelaide, it would be an elder or authorized representative of the Kaurna people. A welcome would normally accompany any *major event*, such as the opening of a new building, a valedictory or graduation ceremony, or the launch of a new program or initiative. To reduce the tendency toward tokenism, settler communities are encouraged to consult with local Indigenous nations at the beginning of any planning towards such initiatives. If local people have been valued and involved from the beginning, a welcome to country will obviously be far more meaningful and offered far more enthusiastically. The form and content of a welcome to country ceremony should be left entirely in the hands of those who will offer it. In any case, it should be the very first thing that happens at any such opening or launch and you should be prepared to negotiate appropriate renumeration for those presiding at the ceremony.

"trawlwulwuy," always in lowercase lettering.

WHAT IS AN "ACKNOWLEDGMENT OF COUNTRY"?

An "Acknowledgment of Country" is a lesser, and considerably briefer, ceremony that should be offered by anyone who is running an event or gathering on the sovereign and unceded lands of Aboriginal or Torres Strait Islander nations. You do not need to be Indigenous yourself to offer such an acknowledgment. Nevertheless, for the sake of integrity, it is best offered within the context of an existing relationship with a local Indigenous group or organization. Obviously, an acknowledgment should still happen even if such a relationship has not been established. Your preparedness to do so can sometimes be a first step in establishing such relations.

Before You Draft Your Acknowledgment

Before you draft an acknowledgment, develop some empathy for the experience of our people. Read our history. Talk with us. Find out about our loss, our grief, our pain. Find out what we long for and what we aspire to. Talk to us about what will best communicate respect. Check if your organization already has an approved form that has been created out of respectful conversation with us. If no such form exists, seeks ways to make that conversation happen. Wherever possible, seek the guidance of Aboriginal and/ or Torres Strait Islander people who are already part of your organization, because they are the ones who will have to listen to your acknowledgment repeatedly. If the acknowledgment doesn't work for them, it doesn't work. If there really are no Aboriginal and/or Torres Strait Islander people in your organization, seek guidance from local mob outside your organization. These days, Aboriginal Controlled Organizations often have websites which will get you started.

If it hasn't happened already, consider starting a conversation in your organization about the ways in which you will collectively work towards greater justice for our mobs within your sphere of activity or influence. This might be in the form of a Justice Action Plan or something similar. Whatever the case, speak only about concrete commitments and the steps to very specific outcomes. Grand and globalizing statements are next to useless.

Drafting the Acknowledgment

An acknowledgment should say something about the land on which you are meeting and the Indigenous group which belongs to that country. Note that this is rarely a group of "traditional owners" in the legal sense, since most mobs do not enjoy complete access to their own lands.

You should acknowledge that the land is unceded (meaning it has never been given away or sold) but was rather taken by colonists in a violent and often genocidal manner. The ancestors who created the land should be acknowledged, because they are the "old people" who still reside in country and speak to us from it. They are the creator guardians, and as close a thing to divinity as mob usually have in our cosmologies. You should then acknowledge the elders who have cared for that country since creation, and who continue to care for country insofar as they are allowed to by colonial authorities. Elders, past and present, have a special responsibility to lead our mobs as we seek to stay connected to country and to our responsibilities as people of the land. Finally, you should give attention to a brief statement of your organization's commitment to a greater justice for our mobs.

Here is a simple example of a general acknowledgment that would do the trick for most churches and church organizations:

> We acknowledge that this church stands on the sovereign and unceded country of the [trawloolway] people, and that this country came into the church's possession by deceitful, murderous, and immoral means. We acknowledge the continuing sovereignty of the [trawloolway] over this country, and the right and responsibility of trawloolway elders, past and present, to care for it according to a wisdom passed down over more than four thousand generations. We give thanks for the ancestors who formed this land and gifted it to the trawloolway to care for. We commit ourselves to work and to pray towards a more just settlement for all Indigenous people.

Here is another example, which exhibits more creativity by referring to some specific features of the country in question:

> We gather today on cold country, the land of the Kulin nations. This is where the luk (eels) navigate the rivers and creeks, the waring (wombats) play amongst the ferns and the wurun (manna gums) stand tall. This the country formed by Bunjil, the great ancestor spirit, and carefully managed by wise arweet (elders) of the Wurundjeri and Bunwurrung clans since the beginning. Today we

give thanks for this country, for the rich and complex communion
of its people, its animals, its plants. And we pause for a moment to
silently pray that future generations will value what has been given
in country far more than it is valued today . . .

Pitfalls to Avoid . . . Please!

If there is a recommended script in your organization that has come out
of an extensive conversation with mob, and has been agreed to by mob,
use it as is. Don't adapt it according to your own wisdom. Just use it. In my
experience, most personal modifications of existing scripts end up insulting or in other ways disrespecting us. Please, please, please, resist that urge.

Please, don't refer to local mobs on country in generic terms. Don't
say, for example, "We meet today on 'Aboriginal'/'Torres Strait Islander'/'K
oori'/'Palawa'/'Murri' country." Doing so shows that you haven't bothered
to find out anything about where you are or whose country it is. This is
deeply insulting.

Please don't refer to mob using possessive phrases such as "our Aboriginal people" or "our Indigenous people." We don't belong to colonists
and never have, except as slaves and indentured servants. Saying that we
belong to you tends to reinforce the fact that we continue to live in a colonial society in which the invaders have most of the power and believe they
have a right to possess us. Again, it is deeply insulting.

Please don't acknowledge "emerging elders." There is no such thing
in Aboriginal or Torres Strait communities. You either are an elder, or you
aren't, and the extensive use of this phrase is really rather annoying.

Please don't refer to "traditional" owners or custodians. This word
does little but reinforce the fact that most of us do not "own" our land in
any legally meaningful sense. It communicates little more than the fact
that, in the eyes of settler law, mob can rarely be more than token owners,
"Clayton's" owners, owners that cannot, in fact, enjoy effective control over
anything at all. It is a word invented and deployed by white lawyers. Please
don't use it.

Speaking of white lawyers, please don't talk about the connection of
mob to land in terms of a period "for," or "since," "time immemorial." This
phrase is another invention of white lawyers, and it infers that we do not
remember who we are and how we are related to our country. The phrase
was invented to represent the fiction that Indigenous peoples do not have a

history that stands up to empirical inquiry: a documentary history, a verifiable history because it is written down on paper, preferably in triplicate, and with the signature of (white) witnesses attached. We do, in fact, remember; we do have a history; we do have a long, long, memory. So, again, this phrase is deeply insulting.

Another feature of many of the acknowledgments we are subjected to is the use of this phrase, or something similar: "We also acknowledge/pay our respects to any Indigenous/Aboriginal/Torres Strait Islander people who may be with us this evening." This kind of thing is insulting on two levels. First, it assumes that a normal gathering of people, or the most usual kind of gathering, does not include mob. This is to normalize the absence of mob from polite, colonial society and therefore reinforce our marginalization and invisibility. Second, the phrase assumes that in the unlikely event that mob might be present, we are only present as a category of people, not as individuals with names or personal agency. This reinforces another strategy beloved of colonial societies: abstraction. A phrase such as this refers to mob in the abstract because abstractions can be dismissed in a way that actual people, with thoughts and feelings and bodies, cannot. So please don't use this phrase in your acknowledgments. If you know that particular mob will be present, and you want to acknowledge the fact publicly, by all means do so. But do it by using our personal names, please. Treat us as people, not as abstractions.

What Theology is Put into Play by Acknowledging Country?

I'm aware that there are Christian communities, most of them from more conservative or even fundamentalist traditions, who object to the use of welcomes to, or acknowledgments of, country in any shape or form. Martin Isles, formerly of the Australian Christian Lobby, released an influential video in 2022 in which he argued that acknowledgments of country are, quite simply, incompatible with Christian faith because they are "pagan": they take as their spiritual starting point the ancestral spirits of the land rather than the triune God made known in Jesus Christ.[3] I would agree with Martin that acknowledgments of country are almost certainly incompatible with Christianity: *if* one understands Christianity as an entirely colonial phenomena, as he does. Obviously, as you will have gathered from reading the earlier chapters of this book, I am not one of those Christians.

3. Isles, "Welcome."

I read the Bible, and much of church tradition, as human attempts to understand the self-revelation of the divine. Sometimes these writers and editors are on to something, sometimes they are not. Sometimes they express themselves in such a way that they can transcend their own cultural baggage and speak to people who belong to other tribes, and sometimes they do not. The important thing to remember, in all of this, is that each attempt to communicate strains towards naming a reality which, in the end, is quite elusive. Elusive because the divine never reveals the totality of its being, but only specific moments or dimensions, and these only ever via the material mediations of people, rituals, and country. Elusive, also, because the human mind simply cannot contain or comprehend that which not only precedes but also exceeds our imaginative capacities. It is far too big and far too glorious, filling every moment and every space at once. "We see now in a mirror, dimly," says St. Paul (1 Cor 13:12), primarily because human beings, unlike the divine reality, fill only one moment in time, and one small space, at once. That does not mean that we cannot see, that we cannot catch glimpses, especially if we are trained to look and to listen well. It does mean, however, that anything we learn of the divine will be necessarily provisional and partial. This ought to incline us towards an attitude of humility in the face of mystery, rather than toward the self-congratulatory triumphalism of the colonial imagination.

To those who worry at Aboriginal and Torres Strait Islander talk of ancestral creator spirits, I would simply remind you of the encounter between Abram—"father" of Jews, Christians, and Muslims—and the priest king of Salem (later called "Jerusalem"). The story is told in Genesis 14:17–24:

> After Abram's return from the defeat of Chedorlaomer and the kings who were with him, the king of Sodom went out to meet him at the Valley of Shaveh (that is, the King's Valley). And King Melchizedek of Salem brought out bread and wine; he was priest of El Elyon. He blessed him and said, "Blessed be Abram by El Elyon, maker of heaven and earth; and blessed be El Elyon, who has delivered your enemies into your hand!"
>
> And Abram gave him one-tenth of everything. Then the king of Sodom said to Abram, "Give me the people, but take the goods for yourself." But Abram said to the king of Sodom, "I have sworn to Yahweh, El Elyon, maker of heaven and earth, that I would not take a thread or a sandal-thong or anything that is yours, so that you might not say, 'I have made Abram rich.' I will take nothing but what the young men have eaten, and the share of the men

who went with me—Aner, Eshcol, and Mamre. Let them take their share." (NRSV adapted)

Here the patriarch not only accepts the blessing of an indigenous priest, a blessing given in the name of a local, entirely Canaanite, deity, but also takes that name to be equivalent to the name of his own god, Yahweh, thus conflating the worship of a Canaanite deity with the worship of Yahweh, the god who will later become the preferred deity of the children of Israel.[4]

I would also remind those who believe that the divine is only divine in a settler-Christian way that the Letter to the Hebrews, which appears in the sacred Scriptures of the New Testament, names Jesus as a priest not in a Christian order, or even in the order of the Aaronic priesthood of the Hebrew people, but in the order of this same Melchizedek, the Canaanite priest:

So also Christ did not glorify himself in becoming a high priest, but was appointed by the one who said to him,

"You are my Son, today I have begotten you";
as he says also in another place,
"You are a priest for ever,
according to the order of Melchizedek." (Heb 5:5–6)

This King Melchizedek of Salem, priest of the Most High God, met Abraham as he was returning from defeating the kings and blessed him; and to him Abraham apportioned "one-tenth of everything." His name, in the first place, means "king of righteousness"; next he is also king of Salem, that is, "king of peace." Without father, without mother, without genealogy, having neither beginning of days nor end of life, but resembling the Son of God, he remains a priest for ever.

See how great he is! Even Abraham the patriarch gave him a tenth of the spoils. And those descendants of Levi who receive the priestly office have a commandment in the law to collect tithes from the people, that is, from their kindred, though these also are descended from Abraham. But this man, who does not belong to their ancestry, collected tithes from Abraham and blessed him who had received the promises.(Heb 7:1–6)

4. These observations are now commonplace in Indigenous theological circles. See, for example, Habel et al., *De-colonising*.

It is even more obvious when another priest arises, resembling Melchizedek, one who has become a priest, not through a legal requirement concerning physical descent, but through the power of an indestructible life. For it is attested of him,
"You are a priest for ever,
according to the order of Melchizedek." (Heb 7:15–17)

Here the writer places Jesus within a matrix of authority which is essentially indigenous rather than Jewish in origin. He is likened to Melchizedek the Canaanite priest, an ancestor without beginning or end, whose authority derives from his participation in the primordial eternity of the divine, rather than in the cult of the Aaronic religious rites. What this means in our own context, I propose, is that Jesus is more creator ancestor than archbishop. He is a figure of country, not of merely churchly rites and successions. I therefore deem it entirely appropriate for Christians to acknowledge the Indigenous spirituality of country from which this form of authority is ultimately derived. It is biblical to do so.

This argument, and therefore the entire argument of this book, is unlikely to satisfy those who believe, at the very bedrock of their preferred ways of encountering the other, that the divine only appears to us in one version, the version supported by a settler-colonial form of Christian language, culture, and cosmology. There is really nothing I can do about that. I leave such people to the divine spirit to deal with. I hope, however, that many who read this book are on the cusp of embracing a wider, at once more inclusive and more complex, version of divine truth; and that anyone who stumbles upon these meditations will be helped and supported in the pilgrimage they have begun to walk.

CHAPTER 9

The Churches, Reconciliation, and Justice

THE RECONCILIATION AGENDA AND ITS DISCONTENTS

What I did not steal must I now restore?(Ps 69:4b)

In the settler colony of Australia, National Reconciliation Week runs from May 27 to June 3 and is immediately preceded by Sorry Day on May 26. The dates are significant. The 1997 report of the Human Rights and Equal Opportunities Commission into the separation of Aboriginal and Torres Strait Islander children from their families, *Bringing Them Home*, was tabled in the federal parliament on May 26. Sorry Day has become an annual observance inviting Australians to reflect on the genocidal policies which sought to destroy Indigenous families and communities and to renew community resolve to avoid ever enacting such policies again.[1] May 27 commemorates the date of the 1967 referendum in which the Australian Constitution was changed to recognize the full membership of Indigenous people in the Commonwealth of Australia[2] and June 3 recalls the 1993 Mabo decision of the High Court of Australia to overturn the racist legal fiction of *terra nullius*.[3] Beginning as a week of "prayer for reconciliation" within some Australian faith communities, the week has now been taken up in some

1. Australian Human Rights Commission, "Past Projects."
2. AIATSIS, "1967 Referendum."
3. AIATSIS, "Mabo Case."

sections of the wider community as a way to encourage the building of bridges between Indigenous and other Australians.[4]

From where I stand, National Reconciliation Week appears to be struggling as a tool to extract a more just settlement for our people, and for two reasons. First, instead of encouraging the colonial establishment to address issues of justice for First Peoples persistently and all year round, National Reconciliation week has become a way in which organizations may signal their virtue and tick a box in this area for one week per year, but effectively ignore our concerns at every other time. Second, it has become increasingly clear that it is Aboriginal and Torres Strait Islander people, not settlers, who are expected to do most of the work of Reconciliation Week, just as we are expected to do most of the work of reconciliation itself. This leads to our elders and prophets growing weary and sad at the lack of progress on justice for our people whilst our colonial governors congratulate themselves for their political virtue. Which leads a great many of us to ask, with the Psalmist, "What I did not steal must I now restore?" Must we who did nothing to create Indigenous suffering now be the ones who must do all the work of healing and restoration? Why cannot those who have benefitted from the dispossession of our people take responsibility for putting things right?

Many others have written about the consequences of conservative government for the reconciliation cause, pointing to the extraordinary lack of progress on matters like treaty, incarceration rates, health outcomes, family integrity, meaningful employment, access to country, housing, and the preservation of language and culture.[5] I don't intend to add to that commentary. Rather, I want to point out that the very churches that initiated the week of prayer for reconciliation have now, very clearly, abandoned the cause in any meaningful sense.

The Uniting Church has long enjoyed a reputation for leading the way on matters of reconciliation. And there are plenty of signs that it continues to do so. Its national constitution has a preamble declaring that First Peoples enjoyed a relationship with the divine prior to the coming of Europeans.[6] The Constitution also recognizes and gives formal institutional authority

---

4. Reconciliation Australia, "What Is?"

5. See, for example, Madison, *Colonial Fantasy.*

6. Not that this Uniting Church divine bears much resemblance to the creator ancestors of traditional Aboriginal and Torres Strait Islander spirituality. See my commentary in chapter 11.

to a national "Congress" of Aboriginal and Torres Strait Islander members of the church who are able to run their own affairs (up to a point).[7] The church funds a small number of Aboriginal and Torres Strait Islander ministries around the nation and has handed some of those ministries land and property for their beneficial use. The church has an interest in a registered training organization, based in Darwin, specifically designed to offer certificate and diploma level education to aspiring First Nations pastors and church workers.[8] In addition, the church each year provides worship and other resources on a "Day of Mourning,"[9] National Reconciliation Week, and NAIDOC Week for the nourishment of its members in the ongoing work of reconciliation. All of which is terrific, at least to the untrained eye.

Of course, as someone who was involved in the Uniting Church as a Congress member for twenty years or so, I can tell you with some experience that the gains of our people over that period were hard won. The church authorities were very good at managing public perceptions, offering fine words of apology and commitment at the very time they were also steadfastly resisting our overtures for greater control of our affairs and a more generous financial investment in our ministries. Many Congress leaders fell into despair and illness as the church hierarchy consistently backed a national leader who was a bully and a criminal. I, myself, eventually left the church because I could not find stable employment and because the battle to find a relatively secure place to stand within the church was making me quite unwell. Behind the glossy presentation of the Uniting Church's leadership on matters of reconciliation there remains a common, everyday racism. I still come across white Uniting Church leaders who have never read a book about the true history of this country, have never had a respectful conversation with an Indigenous person, who have never studied with an Indigenous academic or theologian, and never felt the need to do so. To date, the senior leadership of the church remains overwhelmingly white, and there are no Aboriginal or Torres Strait Islander people on the academic teaching staff of any of its tertiary-level theological colleges. Existing programs in Indigenous theology are few and far between and are not offered as part of recognized degree programs or higher.[10] This serves

---

7. Uniting Church in Australia, "Basis of Union." See Division 4:49.

8. Nungalinya College. "Who Are We?"

9. Uniting Church in Australia. "Day."

10. Uniting College in tarntanya/Adelaide offers a "Walking on Country" program under the leadership of the Reverend Denise Champion, but this is not articulated into a

only to keep Indigenous people, as well as those who might wish to inter-rogate Indigenous knowledges, in a perpetual state of infantilization with respect to Indigenous knowledges.[11] The constant message these certificate programs communicate is that Aboriginal and Torres Strait Islander people are not capable of doing serious theological work and must be subject to the same missionary "correction" of our spiritual knowledges as ever before. Together, these facts lead me to believe that Australia's most progressive church on Aboriginal and Torres Strait Islander matters remains deeply racist both intellectually and practically.

The Roman Catholic Church appears to have both a national and state-based apparatus to address matters of Aboriginal and Torres Strait Islander concern. There is a National Aboriginal and Torres Strait Islander Catholic Council reporting to the Bishop's Conference, and a funded secre-tariat that functions nationally as well as on a state-by-state basis.[12] There is also a Bishop's Commission on Relations with Aboriginal and Torres Strait Islander Peoples, whose mandate includes an aspiration to promote "the full inclusion and participation of Aboriginal and Torres Strait Islander peoples in every aspect of the life of the Church."[13] Most states and territo-ries appear to have at least one funded Indigenous ministry, with lutruwita/Tasmania being a notable exception. In addition, anecdotal evidence would suggest that Catholic schools and welfare agencies often form enthusiastic relationships with Aboriginal organizations and communities, Catholic and otherwise. These bodies collaborate happily both on curriculum and policy materials and on the building of relationships between people from Indig-enous and non-Indigenous backgrounds. The church has also incorporated a national celebration of Aboriginal and Torres Strait Islander people and culture into the liturgical calendar for the first Sunday of July. Certainly, most of the Indigenous Catholics I know are reasonably happy Catholics.

For all this good work, it nevertheless appears that the church has still invested very little into the development of Indigenous theologies, theolo-gians, and clergy. The Roman Church is exemplary in its multiculturalism, not least amongst the clergy. But there are still no Indigenous bishops or tenured theological teachers and no priests. I believe there may be as little

---

degree-level award, as far as I can see. Nungalinya College does not offer courses beyond Certificate 4.

11. For more on this notion, see Nakata, "Infantilisation."

12. NATSICC, "Latest News."

13. Catholic Australia, "Bishops." See section 2.4 of the mandate.

as three active deacons. As far as I can tell, there have been no attempts by the church to develop a sophisticated theological paradigm which takes Indigenous knowledges seriously.[14] Whilst the church has claimed several Indigenous lay leaders as its own, the work of these people is usually celebrated for its practical contribution to settler society rather than for its theological or spiritual value to the church. Obvious examples would be the late Aunty Betty Pike, who wrote a book on spirituality,[15] and educationalist, Aunty Miriam Ungunmerr-Bauman, whose article on "Dadirri" has been domesticated to the point of caricature in most Catholic circles.[16] There are still, in other words, almost no Indigenous voices where official policy might be affected, amongst the pastoral and teaching authorities of the church. The recent Plenary Council of the Australian Catholic Church did not advance this situation.[17]

The Anglican Church of Australia, likewise, has established a National Aboriginal and Torres Strait Islander Anglican Council, which reports to the General Synod under what is known as the NATSIAC canon.[18] This council, of which I am currently a member, consists of a National Aboriginal and a National Torres Strait Islander bishop appointed by the Primate, plus representatives appointed by the twenty-three diocesan bishops of the church, along with up to ten representatives elected by NATSIAC itself. The dioceses of the Northern Territory, Northwest Australia, North Queensland, and Brisbane may appoint more than one representative (up to six, in one instance) because the church perhaps believes that these are more Indigenous places. Several bishops apparently do not get around to appointing anyone at all and some appoint non-Indigenous people (which the canon does not explicitly forbid). The General Synod, whilst allowing NATSIAC to raise its own funds, contributes a very small amount from its annual budget to fund a part-time secretariat and the attendance at council of representatives from the north of the continent. Other dioceses are

14. The Roman Catholic Church partners in Nungalinya College as well. But, as noted with the Uniting Church, Nungalinya does not teach Indigenous approaches to theology at a tertiary level. This effectively keeps the Indigenous leadership of the church out of mainstream theological work.

15. Pike, *Power*.

16. See my discussion of the notion in chapter 4.

17. The final decree of the council is exceptionally vague on matters of theology, liturgy, and formation in an Aboriginal or Torres Strait Islander mode. See Plenary Council, "Reconciliation."

18. NATSIAC, "Members." See also NATSIAC, "Canon."

expected to fund the attendance at council of their own representatives, which is presumably part of the reason why some dioceses do not send anyone.

The provision of Aboriginal or Torres Strait Islander ministry in the Anglican church is deeply problematic. I am not aware of a diocese in which there are specific provisions for the employment of Indigenous ministers toward Indigenous ministries. Across the church, nationally, it would be fair to say that almost all Indigenous church workers, ordained or not, engage in ministry with, or on behalf of, our people on our own time and at our own expense. The number of funded Aboriginal or Torres Strait Islander ministries can be counted on one hand. The Anglican Board of Mission is allowed by its charter to fund individual projects that engage with Indigenous peoples, but that same charter prohibits the funding of wages or stipends, which effectively means that ABM cannot support Indigenous ministers, lay or ordained, to do long-term embedded ministries in Aboriginal or Torres Strait Islander communities. Ironically, ABM seems to be able to employ white "missioners" who are supposed to engage with our mobs, just not Indigenous ministers. It is sobering to note, in addition, that whilst the Primate of the church can appoint national bishops for both the Aboriginal and Torres Strait Islander communities, there is currently no funding allocated to do so by the national church. The national Torres Strait Islander episcopate has therefore been vacant for almost two decades, and the national Aboriginal episcopate is currently being funded on a part-time basis by Anglicare in South Australia.

One might additionally note that pleas for a more meaningful engagement from the Anglican Church usually fall on deaf ears. Since its establishment in 1998, the National Aboriginal and Torres Strait Islander Anglican Council has sought on multiple occasions both a meaningful covenant or treaty with the rest of the church, and a more substantial funding base to underwrite its aspirations. Neither have been forthcoming. And, as with the Roman Catholic and Uniting Churches, it is still the case that there is no secure and ongoing Indigenous presence in the mainstream theological colleges of the church, and less than a handful of Indigenous voices on diocesan councils in the whole of Australia. The church participates in two TAFE-level training institutes for Indigenous peoples,[19] but these are subject to the same issues of infantilization I've noted with the Roman Catholic

19. Nungalinya College in Darwin, as previously mentioned, and Wontulp-Bi-Buya College in Cairns. Wontulp-Bi-Buya College, "Celebrating."

and Uniting Churches. This writer can only conclude that reconciliation in the sense of restoring some measure of voice, dignity, and justice to First Peoples is effectively terminal in the Anglican Church.

Notwithstanding these realities, church communities routinely call on mob in National Reconciliation Week or in NAIDOC Week to participate in symbolic acts of reconciliation, usually within the context of worship services run by white people who appear to be engaged in virtue signaling. More often than not, the invitation arrives just a few days before the proposed event because that is how long that congregation has allocated to planning. There is no preexisting relationship with this church. There has been no foregoing process of story sharing or relationship building, out of which the event or worship service might gather to itself some genuine meaning for the participating community. Furthermore, precisely because of the lack of conversation with the congregation in question, one cannot help but feel that there will be little to no positive outcome from the event for our people. There will be no commitments made, for example, to hand back some land, or pay the rent, or fund an Indigenous ministry, or engage in ongoing conversation with an Aboriginal or Torres Strait Islander organization. To make those kinds of outcomes even remotely possible requires a long conversation, much education, and the fundamental conversion of racist hearts and minds. All a one-off event can usually achieve is a self-congratulatory feeling of virtue in the hosting organization for broaching such "complex" issues.

These realities leave us Indigenous Christian leaders in a place of considerable dilemma. Most of us have been seeking to modify the scorn, ignorance, and indifference in our churches, the churches we love, for decades. We are therefore deeply skeptical about the value of doing what is asked of us. Yet we feel we have a responsibility to our people, especially our kids, to keep speaking out, to keep fighting the fight as our elders did before us at great personal cost, even though it is so very, very difficult to sustain doing so. So, we pull ourselves together, put on a smiling face, turn up, do our little bit, and hope for the best. We pray that our ancestors will give us patience to answer all the hurtful and disrespectful questions without losing our cool. And we go home even more exhausted, and usually just a little bit despairing at the fact that the questions have not changed for decades. Despite all this, or most probably because of it, I am a person of prayer. I pray not because I am serene. I pray because I am desperate. Without the water from the well, which is the word of the suffering and resurrected

Christ which I find in country, I would surely succumb to the floods of despair with which I am overcome at every reconciliation event. "Help me ancestors, help me Jesus, to stay alive, that the longing for your justice and peace may stay alive in me." That is my prayer, and most days—especially during Reconciliation Week—that is about the best I can do.

The fundamental difficulty here, it seems to me, is that the churches expect that Indigenous people ought to wipe the record of the past clean with an all-inclusive act of forgiveness. But this expectation is both cruel and unrealistic. Forgiveness is something that can only be offered freely and despite all reasonable expectation; it cannot be commanded or coerced from traumatized and wronged victims. A coerced act of forgiveness is not forgiveness. It is a contractual exchange in which one party surrenders both its truth and its reasonable expectations toward reparation and healing to buy very limited forms of favor from a powerful patron. There is nothing good or gracious about that. To capitulate to the more powerful foe in this manner does little else than to guarantee that the pain, the victim blaming, and the abuse will continue in perpetuity.

This prevailing doctrine of forgiveness routinely skips a crucial step, a step we Anglicans call "repentance and amendment of life" on the part of those who perpetuate the wrongs. Repentance cannot be reduced to saying sorry. Repentance requires doing everything humanly possible to unweave the injustice committed, to give back what was stolen, to bind up the wounds, to restore what was broken. Now, obviously, not all can be restored. Not all can be healed. Not all can be repaired. But repentance requires that everything that can be done, is done. Without this desire and this real, concrete action, sorry is just a word, a word that fails to become incarnate, to take flesh, to inhabit the real world as the practice of justice.

THE LAW, THE PROPHETS, AND JUSTICE FOR FIRST PEOPLES

In the Gospel of Matthew, Jesus says:

> Do not think that I have come to abolish the law or the prophets; I have come not to abolish but to fulfill. For truly I tell you, until heaven and earth pass away, not one letter, not one stroke of a letter, will pass from the law until all is accomplished. Therefore, whoever breaks one of the least of these commandments, and teaches others to do the same, will be called least in the kingdom

of heaven; but whoever does them and teaches them will be called great in the kingdom of heaven. For I tell you, unless your justice exceeds that of the scribes and Pharisees, you will never enter the kingdom of heaven. (Matt 5:17–20)

So, what is this "law" that Jesus does not intend to abolish, and who are these "prophets" whose oracles Jesus intends to fulfill? The law is the law of Moses, the law given to Israel after they have fled slavery in Egypt, the ten words or commandments. You can read about them in Exodus chapter 20. Amongst the laws are these:

You shall have no gods before Yahweh.
You shall not worship idols.
Keep the sabbath.
You shall not murder.
You shall not steal.
You shall not bear false witness against your neighbor.
You shall not covet what belongs to your neighbor.

"Do not think, for one moment," says the Matthean Jesus, "that I have come to do away with this law. I have not. This law will stand until the age has reached its conclusion. Keep this law, and you will be called great in the kingdom of heaven. Break this law, and you will be called the least in the kingdom of heaven." The law stands, then. It has not been swept away by some cheap and unnuanced understanding of "grace" or "forgiveness," as some seem to believe. It stands. And you and I, who believe in the teaching of Jesus, are called to keep it.

The prophets, whose oracles the Matthean Jesus came to fulfill, bear witness to the importance of the law. This law provided the foundation from which Isaiah, for example, passed judgment on the nobles and landowners of Israel in the eighth century BCE:

"Why do we fast, but you do not see?
    Why humble ourselves, but you do not notice?"
Look, you serve your own interest on your fast-day,
    and oppress all your workers.
Look, you fast only to quarrel and to fight
    and to strike with a wicked fist.
Such fasting as you do today
    will not make your voice heard on high.
Is such the fast that I choose,
    day to humble oneself?

Is it to bow down the head like a bulrush,
>   and to lie in sackcloth and ashes?
Will you call this a fast,
>   a day acceptable to the Lord?
Is not this the fast that I choose:
>   to loose the bonds of injustice,
>   to undo the thongs of the yoke,
to let the oppressed go free,
>   and to break every yoke?
Is it not to share your bread with the hungry,
>   and bring the homeless poor into your house;
when you see the naked, to cover them,
>   and not to hide yourself from your own kin?
Then your light shall break forth like the dawn,
>   and your healing shall spring up quickly;
your vindicator shall go before you,
>   the glory of the Lord shall be your rearguard.
Then you shall call, and the Lord will answer;
>   you shall cry for help, and he will say, Here I am.
If you remove the yoke from among you,
>   the pointing of the finger, the speaking of evil,
if you offer your food to the hungry
>   and satisfy the needs of the afflicted,
then your light shall rise in the darkness
>   and your gloom be like the noonday.
>   (Isa 58:4–10)

The prophet here criticizes the wealthy for abandoning the law of God in three respects. First, they steal from their own workers, those who labor in their farms and vineyards. They cheat their workers of their just wages. Second, they tell lies about one another and plan violent assaults upon one another in the hope of securing the wealth that belongs to their neighbors. Third, they are content to allow the hungry in their communities to remain hungry. They will not share their plenty with those who are poor through no fault of their own. They will not take such folk into their homes and tend their wounds. They remain aloof and uncaring. Thus, in these three respects, the wealthy are chided by the prophet for their lack of neighborly care. For a neighbor who cares will not steal; a neighbor who cares will not lie and plan violence against others; a neighbor who cares will not hoard what they have and fail to share it with those who have nothing.

In the Gospel of Matthew, Jesus is like a new Moses, a new Isaiah. He is Moses come from Egypt to give the law again. He is Isaiah come to warn the wealthy Jewish collaborators with the Roman Empire that their greed and indifference will result only in their ruin. "Why," he says, "can you not be like salt, which gives a meal its tang, and makes it attractive?" "Why," he says, "can you not be like a light on a hill, paragons of justice that inspire others to be good, and to love, and to take mind of one's neighbors?' (Matt 5:13–15). These are exactly the questions that face us as churches and as a commonwealth.

Australia is a nation that has become powerful by coveting, stealing, murdering, and slaving: coveting Aboriginal and Torres Strait Islander territories, murdering those who sought to defend it, annexing those territories, and carrying our children off into slavery and domestic servitude. Our churches, with a few local exceptions, worked hand in glove with the colonial authorities. Those who did the stealing, the murdering, and the slaving were overwhelmingly Christians. And it was church-run missions and orphanages that enabled and participated in the destruction of language and culture, the separation of families and the training and placement of children into domestic servitude.[20]

That is why Aboriginal and Torres Strait Islander Australia is in such distress, even now. It is why we are the most incarcerated people on the planet.[21] It is why our kids take their own lives at rates unrivalled by any other people group in Australia.[22] It is why we regularly die in the custody of justice officials but no one has ever—ever!—been held accountable for such deaths.[23] It is why we still have so little ownership or control of our own lives or the land that was given to us by our ancestors. It is why most of us remain sick and poor.[24] All because church and state broke every single one of those commandments that Jesus came to teach and to fulfill. All because the church failed in the duty to be a neighbor.

For thirty years, I have seen the church pray for Aboriginal people. I have seen the church say sorry to Aboriginal people. And, as detailed earlier in this chapter, I've seen the church set up Aboriginal councils, "Voices," if you will, to advise synods and bishop's councils on what to do

20. Again, I refer the reader to this historical record as brought to light in such works as: Rintoul, *Wailing*; Boyce, *Van Diemen's Land*; *1835*; Harris, *One Blood*; and Curthoys and Mitchell, *Liberty*.

21. Anthony, "FactCheck."

22. Dudgeon and Hirvonen, "Why?"

23. Taylor, "Indigenous."

24. As reported in the latest "Closing the Gap" report commissioned by the Commonwealth and published in November 2022. NIAA, "Commonwealth."

about the Aboriginal "problem." What I have not seen in those thirty years, however, is a church that will do anything much at all about justice, about the fulfilling of the law and the prophets after the way of Jesus. I have not seen a church hand back its stolen land. I have not seen a church compensate the families of those whose children it took away and sent into slavery or domestic servitude. I have never seen a church do positive things to reverse the trends: set binding Aboriginal employment benchmarks, for example, or place real power in the hands of mob to do things our way. I have not seen the church do any of these neighborly things. I have not seen a church that can even begin to understand what costly love might require. I have only seen a church of "thoughts and prayers," of words and glossy brochures.

In this way the tragedy of the church in this place, in this country, is directly related to the tragedy of my people. By failing to be the church—to love the neighbor rather than murder, rape, and steal from the neighbor—the church guarantees that its neighbor will suffer rather than thrive. At the same time, the church continues to carry the guilt of its original sin, and so fails to thrive in being genuinely "salty" or a light for the nations.

But the good news is this: the story of our churches and our commonwealth is not yet complete; it is not yet over. We have the power, together, to change the story. Remember those words from Isaiah 58:9b–10:

> If you remove the yoke from among you, the pointing of the finger, the speaking of evil, if you offer your food to the hungry and satisfy the needs of the afflicted, then your light shall rise in the darkness and your gloom be like the noonday.

As we prepare for the referendum on the Aboriginal and Torres Strait Islander Voice to Parliament, there is before us yet another opportunity for the churches to turn around, to forsake their evils, and to walk the way of Christ; to embrace a far more thoroughgoing fast. If they so chose, the churches could do some measure of justice, so that the oppressed can begin their long walk to freedom. For in the freedom of Indigenous peoples is the freedom of people of faith. In the liberation of those whom the churches have long repressed is their own liberation.

So, write to your churchly leaders if you have a care. Implore them to do justice on your behalf. Write to your national leaders and implore them to take care of the First Peoples of this land. Implore them all to make treaty with us, to enact a more just settlement that may finally enable a healing of the wounds that rend us all. If you do this, your churchly light will finally rise and the gloom that afflicts us all will be replaced by the brightness of your dawn.

CHAPTER 10

On Mourning, the Crown, and Anglican Coloniality

In the weeks following September 8, 2022, when Queen Elizabeth II of Britain died, the Australian media covered its aftermath in church and state on a 24/7 basis. The coverage was total, a veritable tsunami of reporting on the minutiae of royal goings-on, along with opinion pieces in their hundreds on the Crown, its legacy, rituals, and future. The ABC, our national broadcaster, even required its presenters to don black as a sign of sorrow.

If it was never clear before, it is clear now: we are a colony. Our head of state is the sovereign of Great Britain. Our politicians, along with our judicial and military officers, swear their allegiance to that sovereign. The legislation generated by our parliaments requires royal assent. When the Queen died, our Prime Minister suspended parliament and declared a National Day of Mourning, to be observed on Thursday the 22nd of September. He, the Governor General, the Leader of the Opposition, and a carefully selected group of prominent Australians, attended the Queen's funeral in London. We are a colony.

Most people I know personally, regardless of ethnicity and origin, seem able to distinguish between a certain sympathy for the royal family and the British people in their grief and loss, and the Crown as an institution and arch symbol of empire. This distinction enables them to generate real feeling for those who mourn, without, at the same time, losing the capacity for critical assessment when it comes to the brutal legacy of the Crown both at home and in the colonies.

I'm aware of many others, however, who will abide no critique at all, who see every word of critical analysis as an attack on the person of Queen Elizabeth herself. Much of this sensitivity comes, in my observation, out of a belief that her late Majesty was a person of exemplary moral integrity who (unlike some members of her extended family) could do no wrong. This moral integrity is then able to, through some syllogism of the imagination which I struggle to comprehend, cover the institution of the Crown as well. Elizabeth was good. The Crown was Elizabeth. Therefore, the Crown is good. Something like that.

Several commentators[1] point out that the imputed "goodness" and homely "ordinariness" of the Queen is not something that can be easily and independently established. For the almost hagiographic image we have of the Queen is most likely that which the Crown, and the Crown alone, has sought to project. The Queen's image, in other words, has been carefully constructed by the Crown over decades with the willing complicity of Her Majesty's Government and the world's most influential media. In fact, very few people know the Queen as a person in much depth at all. And those people are most unlikely, given the position of the Crown at the apex of power in Britain, to offer a counternarrative that will successfully "cut through" into the public imagination.

The "goodness" of the Queen as a person, insofar as that can be independently established, contrasts rather starkly, however, with the institution of the Crown, which is clearly and incontestably one of the most evil and exploitative institutions to have ever walked this earth. Even if one were inclined to separate the Crown from the actions of the British government during the colonial period—during which millions of Indigenous peoples had lives, lands, and material cultures stolen at the point of a gun—there can be no doubt that the Crown has benefited enormously from such exploitations. Forbes estimates the Queen's personal wealth at something like $500 million US and the total assets of the Crown at roughly $28 billion US. Amongst the many assets personally belonging to the Queen (and now to King Charles III) are artefacts—jewellery, for example—stolen from the colonies. Significantly, the Crown pays no land, capital gains or inheritance tax. And it receives substantial salaries for the principal royals from the government of the day.[2]

---

1. For example: Owens, *Family Firm*; Hitchens, *Monarchy*; and Brown, *Palace Papers*.
2. Shapiro and Çam, "Inside."

The distinction, if there is one, between the person who was Queen Elizabeth and the Crown as the primary symbol and beneficiary of an empire that raped, murdered, and pillaged its way across the globe, also seems largely lost on Anglicans, even Australian Anglicans. Of course, I can understand members of the Church of England doing so. For they are bedfellows, with the Crown, in the Establishment. Their bishops sit in the House of Lords and their monarch is the "Supreme Governor" of the Church of England, who must assent to the appointment of any new bishop. This means, amongst other things, that the church is required to preside at many of the key ceremonies of state: weddings, funerals, coronations, and the like. It also means that the church is culturally attached to the Crown. Its official liturgy encourages prayers for the sovereign to be said at least weekly. And the royal anthem, "God save the King," a victory song of empire, is regularly sung in ceremonies presided over by the church.

I was naively unprepared, however, for dealing with the extent to which this liturgical royalism also pertains to Australia, and to the Anglican Church of Australia. Apparently, many Anglican cathedrals are quite happy to accede to the expectations of state, and especially of governors and governors-general, when it comes to the celebration of the Crown. St. Paul's Anglican Cathedral in Melbourne, for example, held a service of "Solemn Choral Evensong to give thanks for the life of Her Majesty Elizabeth II" which was attended by the Premier and the Governor of Victoria, along with many civil servants. Bishops and cathedral deans from elsewhere in Victoria also participated in the service. The usual service of evening prayer was modified, in this instance, to include the following:

- a lowering of the Aboriginal flag, at the entrance to the cathedral, to half-mast along with the flag of the Commonwealth of Australia

- a modification of the usual acknowledgment of country to exclude any reference to Aboriginal sovereignty or the illegitimacy of colonial annexation of Kulin land. The usual affirmation to work for a "more just settlement for Indigenous people" was also removed

- the singing of two colonial victory songs at the conclusion of the service: the national anthem of Australia (which, as we have seen, declares and celebrates the doctrine of *terra nullius*) and the "royal anthem" (which celebrates the sovereignty of the Crown in the territories of empire, and the victory of the sovereign over his/her enemies).

As an Aboriginal member of the Cathedral congregation these modifications shook me considerably. For the Cathedral administration made it clear, in this instance, that a relationship with the state and its expectations was of more importance than a relationship with us and our aspirations towards justice. In conversation with the dean afterward, it also became clear that he regretted that this was so and was open to a conversation about doing things rather differently the next time around. Still, the status quo became starkly and alarmingly clear in this moment and, as I write, many Anglican churches have just put on special services to celebrate the coronation of Charles III.

Of course, I have no objection to Christian people praying for the British royal family and the British people in their grief or their joy. I'm just somewhat flabbergasted that a church which makes no mention whatsoever of the British Crown in its constitution would want to celebrate that Crown in ways that so unfeelingly rub British coloniality in the faces of those of us who have suffered most at its hand. Particularly, I might say, in a service of evening prayer in which the revolutionary words of the *Magnificat* (as recorded in the Book of Common Prayer) are regularly sung:

> He hath put down the mighty from their seat:
> and hath exalted the humble and meek.
> He hath filled the hungry with good things:
> and the rich he hath sent empty away.

I'm aware, also, that the St. Paul's service was by no means the worst example of such ongoing obeisance. There were many others, services in congregations the land over, that went (and will go) much, much further in their royal fervor. One example is a "Requiem Eucharist for Her Late Majesty, Queen Elizabeth II" held on Sunday morning, September 11, 2022, at St. John's Church in Malvern, Victoria. In addition to the inclusion of the royal anthem, this service also displaced the ordinary for the day from *A Prayer Book for Australia* and included an intercession for "our Sovereign Lord, the King." There was no acknowledgment of country whatsoever. The vicar of that congregation often refers to the royals, in social media posts, as "their sacred majesties."

These liturgical outbreaks of colonialism in fact reflect a deeper and more difficult problem in the Anglican Church: it's almost complete disregard for Aboriginal and Torres Strait Islander people and our attempts to be part of the church—not as honorary whites, but as ourselves. Despite guarded acknowledgments of the church's willing partnership in the genocidal actions of the Crown in days gone by, the church struggles to do anything meaningful when it comes to designing a more inclusive and just future.

Yes, as noted in the last chapter, the church has NATSIAC, a national council of Aboriginal and Torres Strait Islander people. But this body is massively underfunded and has no constitutional or practical power to do anything else than meet. Individual dioceses, and the General Synod itself, can completely ignore what it says, and regularly do. Most of the members of NATSIAC are also appointed by diocesan bishops rather than elected by Aboriginal and Torres Strait Islander people. And the numbers are heavily weighted toward the north of the continent, where so many of our people still live out of a "mission mentality" when it comes to relationships with the church. These factors mean that NATSIAC remains a fundamentally conservative body when compared with the more progressive work of Indigenous organizations outside the church.

And, yes, we have a National Aboriginal Bishop and upwards of twenty deacons and priests around the colony, a tiny percentage of the whole. But most of those priests and deacons work in mainstream white or multicultural congregations, because there are few mechanisms in the Anglican Church for supporting us to work in communities with higher proportions of Indigenous people, or even to work on special projects seeking to progress the fortunes of our people in the church. Those who work in majority Indigenous communities, for example, are rarely paid. They depend upon additional non-church jobs or, where eligible, government pensions to put food on the table. The National Aboriginal Bishop, himself, is funded for two days per week. Two days to offer care and encouragement to Aboriginal leaders across the entire continent. Two days! And, despite the NATSIAC canon making provision for one, there has not been a National Torres Strait Islander Bishop in decades. Apparently, the money is simply not there (church-speak for "not a priority").

So, we are a do-nothing church when it comes to improving the lives and meaningful participation of Aboriginal and Torres Strait Islander people. If the church really cared for us, it would gather the resources to do at least some of the following:

- pay our clergy a just stipend to care for our own Aboriginal and Torres Strait Islander people, wherever they might be

- mandate the presence of Aboriginal and Torres Strait Islander voices in every council or board of every Anglican organization or diocese in the colony

- fully fund both a National Aboriginal Bishop and a National Torres Strait Islander Bishop

- fully fund NATSIAC (with staff and a secretariat) as a hub for ministry and leadership development for our people

- mandate the teaching of Indigenous theologies in our clergy training institutions

- mandate the teaching of Indigenous knowledges in our schools

- fund the development, authorization, and dissemination of liturgical resources which reflect a First Peoples perspective and experience

- hand properties gifted to the church by the Crown back to local Aboriginal or Torres Strait Islander custodians.

That would be a good start. In the Province of Victoria, Aboriginal clergy put such initiatives on the table of provincial and diocesan councils back in 2018. We invited the councils of the church to sit down with us to discuss the possibility of a covenant or agreement that would represent a more just settlement for our people. Neither diocesan councils, nor the provincial council, have yet troubled to respond to that invitation.[3]

"How could such ministries be funded?" I hear you ask. By asking congregations, church organizations, and dioceses to "pay the rent" on stolen land by contributing a percentage of their annual budgets to recognized Aboriginal and Torres Strait Islander ministries. By returning lands granted to churches by the Crown to those from who that land was stolen. And by contributing a proportion of all property sales to recognized Indigenous ministries.

We could do this, if we wanted to—if we really and truly believed in justice rather than in the continuing sovereignty of the Crown over those whom it dispossessed.

---

3. Part of that story can be read in this resolution to the Melbourne synod from 2019: Deverell, "Next Steps."

Chapter 11

Colonizing Indigenous Religion?

A Case Study from the Uniting Church in Australia[1]

The *Preamble to the Constitution of the Uniting Church in Australia* raises several questions concerning the nature and authority of theological formulations within the conversation between Indigenous people and settler colonial Christians. On what basis can anyone claim to know that the Triune God of Uniting Church Christians is *the same as* the creator ancestors who formed the Australian landscape and speaks through Aboriginal and Torres Strait Islander law, custom, and ceremony? Is it appropriate, in an intellectual milieu seeking to address its invasive coloniality, to claim that Jesus Christ is the *final and full revelation* of divine love and grace? This chapter seeks to untangle these and related questions as a case study in the as yet barely underway conversation between black, white, and Indigenous theologians about the status of Christ in "postcolonial" discourse.[2]

---

1. A draft of this chapter was first aired at the "Intellectual Authority and its Changing Infrastructures in North American and Australian Christianity" symposium, jointly sponsored by Deakin University, the Religious History Association and Australian Catholic University, on July 8–9, 2021.

2. Prominent examples of pioneering work in this conversation include: Jennings, *Christian Imagination*, Woodley, *Indigenous Theology*, Brett, *Locations*, and Deverell, *Gondwana*.

THEOLOGICAL CLAIMS FROM THE PREAMBLE TO THE CONSTITUTION OF THE UNITING CHURCH

After a two-decade long conversation between settler and Indigenous members of the Uniting Church in Australia, in July 2009 the national Assembly of the Uniting Church in Australia passed a resolution to amend the church's constitution by affixing a preamble which includes the following:

> As the Church believes that God guided it into union so it believes God is calling it to continually seek a renewal of its life as a community of First Peoples and of Second Peoples from many lands, and as part of that to RECOGNISE THAT:
>
> 1. When the churches that formed the Uniting Church arrived in Australia as part of the process of colonisation they entered a land that had been created and sustained by the Triune God they knew in Jesus Christ.
>
> 2. Through this land God had nurtured and sustained the First Peoples of this country, the Aboriginal and Islander peoples, who continue to understand themselves to be the traditional owners and custodians (meaning "sovereign" in the language of the First Peoples) of these lands and waters since time immemorial.
>
> 3. The First Peoples had already encountered the Creator God before the arrival of the colonisers; the Spirit was already in the land revealing God to the people through law, custom and ceremony. The same love and grace that was finally and fully revealed in Jesus Christ sustained the First Peoples and gave them particular insights into God's ways.
>
> 4. Some members of the uniting churches approached the First Peoples with good intentions, standing with them in the name of justice; considering their well being, culture and language as the churches proclaimed the reconciling purpose of the Triune God found in the good news about Jesus Christ.
>
> 5. Many in the uniting churches, however, shared the values and relationships of the emerging colonial society including paternalism and racism towards the First Peoples. They were complicit in the injustice that resulted in many of the First People being dispossessed from their land, their language, their culture and spirituality, becoming strangers in their own land.
>
> 6. The uniting churches were largely silent as the dominant culture of Australia constructed and propagated a distorted version of

history that denied this land was occupied, utilised, cultivated and harvested by these First Peoples who also had complex systems of trade and inter-relationships. As a result of this denial, relationships were broken, and the very integrity of the Gospel proclaimed by the churches was diminished.

7. From the beginning of colonisation the First Peoples challenged their dispossession and the denial of their proper place in this land. In time, this was taken up in the community, in the courts, in the parliaments, in the way history was recorded and told, and in the Uniting Church in Australia.

8. In 1985 Aboriginal and Torres Strait Islander members of the Uniting Church in Australia formed the Uniting Aboriginal and Islander Christian Congress.

9. In 1988 the Aboriginal and Islander Christian Congress invited the other members of the Church to join in a solemn act of covenanting before God.

10. After much struggle and debate, in 1994 the Assembly of the Uniting Church discovered God's call, accepted this invitation and entered into an ever deepening covenantal relationship with the Uniting Aboriginal and Islander Christian Congress. This was so that all would see a destiny together, praying and working together for a fuller expression of our reconciliation in Jesus Christ.

AND THUS the Church celebrates this Covenantal relationship as a foretaste of that coming reconciliation and renewal which is the end in view for the whole creation.[3]

I quote this section of the constitution in full because it is important that readers hear the rhetorical and storytelling cadences of the preamble. In many ways, the preamble functions like the ecumenical creeds of the church catholic in that it not only tells a story which has a beginning, a middle, and an end, but it also seeks to map out the characteristics of a Uniting Church orthodoxy over and against various groups of imagined dissenters. Amidst the many legitimate ways in which the preamble might be exegeted, the reflections that follow will confine themselves to a consideration of theological matters.[4] Specifically, I will seek to name and interrogate the characters, times, places, and relationships at play in the preamble's

3. Uniting Church in Australia, *Basis of Union*, 41–42.

4. For a fulsome set of responses utilizing a variety of academic methods, I refer the reader to Uniting Church in Australia, *New Preamble*.

theological story concerning an "Australian" version of the Triune God and conclude that this story succeeds only to reproduce the very coloniality the authors apparently intended to overcome. I'll finish the chapter with a modest, and hardly original, proposal towards a better telling of the story by deploying, once again, a christological aesthetic of country.

ANALYSIS AND CRITIQUE

So, let's begin with the characters in the story. The first character to appear is "the church." The "church" named here is neither a specific local congregation of Christians, nor is it the church universal. It is the Uniting Church in Australia, a 1977 union of Congregational, Methodist, and Presbyterian churches that claims in its *Basis of Union* to live and work "within the faith and unity of the One Holy Catholic and Apostolic Church."[5] Note the spatial language in this description. The Uniting Church is located both "in Australia" and "within" the universal church. Theologically, as we shall see later, these spatial containers may, in fact, work against each other. "Australia" is a colonial fiction created by white Europeans, whilst the church catholic is, theologically at least, a multiethnic container for the Jewish Jesus.

Which brings us to a second character in this story, "God" or the "Triune God" (the names are used interchangeably). We may presume from contextual evidence that the God being referred to here is the Trinitarian God of the ecumenical creeds, for the *Basis of Union* of the Uniting Church names its use of the Apostles' and Nicene Creeds as a significant site of its unity with the church catholic.[6] In that same document, the Uniting Church names God as a "Father" who sends his son, the "Lord Jesus Christ," into the world in order to reconcile that world to his Father. It also says that "God in Christ has given to men in the Church the Holy Spirit as a pledge and foretaste of that coming reconciliation and renewal, which is the end in view for the whole creation."[7] What this God primarily does in the world, according to this founding document, is reconcile sinners to himself and create the church as a community of reconciliation.[8]

If we turn to the way this mission of God is described in the preamble, we find that God calls the Uniting Church to "continually seek a renewal of

5. Uniting Church in Australia, *Basis of Union*, 9.
6. Uniting Church in Australia, *Basis of Union*, 12.
7. Uniting Church in Australia, *Basis of Union*, 10.
8. Uniting Church in Australia, *Basis of Union*, 10.

its life as a community of First Peoples and of Second Peoples from many lands."[9] Presumably this is at least one of the ways in which God makes the church into a community of reconciliation. We read here that God is the creator and sustainer of the lands called "Australia" and had "nurtured and sustained" the "Aboriginal and Islander" peoples before the arrival of colonizers.[10] Yes, the Spirit of God was already in the land before colonizers arrived, revealing the Triune God to native peoples through "law, custom and ceremony." Apparently the "very same love and grace that was finally and fully revealed in Jesus Christ sustained the First Peoples and gave them particular insights into God's ways."[11]

I imagine these claims could be read as an exegesis of that statement of St. Paul, in Romans 1:19–20a, which is very commonly seen as the foundation for what is called "natural theology":

> For what can be known about God is plain to them, because God has shown it to them. Ever since the creation of the world his eternal power and divine nature, invisible though they are, have been understood and seen through the things he has made.

Here the apostle has been read to say that at least some of what might be known about God—even though these things are "invisible"—can be understood through the things God has made, through giving one's attention to the creation itself. If that is the case, then let me proceed to introduce the third character in our *dramatis personae*: the "First Peoples," Aboriginal and Islander peoples of Australia. It is the First Peoples whom God apparently teaches about Godself before the colonists first arrived from Europe.

Here I must immediately flag a couple of serious theological problems. First, it isn't clear from the Pauline passage in Romans 1 that the people who may know God from the works of God in creation include either Indigenous people in general or Aboriginal and Islander people in particular. Verse 18 identifies the recipients of this general revelation only as "those who by their wickedness suppress the truth," presumably both "Greeks" and "barbarians" as verse 14 would have it. "Greeks" in the Pauline corpus are usually the citizens of the Roman Empire, whilst "barbarians" are those who threaten the empire from just outside its bounds. Hardly Indigenes from as far away as Oceania, or even the Americas. These faraway worlds,

---

9. Uniting Church in Australia, *Basis of Union*, 40.

10. Uniting Church in Australia, *Basis of Union*, 40–41.

11. Uniting Church in Australia, *Basis of Union*, 41.

and especially the religious and spiritual practices of their inhabitants, could not have been imagined by this worldly Jew from the Mediterranean rim. Including these worlds within the apostles' purview, as the preamble does, would therefore require a significant deployment of interpretive analogy, which, while not problematic in itself, clearly becomes so when one notices that the primary characteristic of the Greeks and barbarians, for St. Paul, is their wickedness:

> So they are without excuse; for though they knew God, they did not honor him as God or give thanks to him, but they became futile in their thinking, and their senseless minds were darkened. Claiming to be wise, they became fools; and they exchanged the glory of the immortal God for images resembling a mortal human being or birds or four-footed animals or reptiles. Therefore God gave them up in the lusts of their hearts to impurity, to the degrading of their bodies among themselves, because they exchanged the truth about God for a lie and worshipped and served the creature rather than the Creator, who is blessed for ever! Amen. (Rom 1:20b–25)

It is difficult to discern the presence of the preamble's "First Peoples" here, even if one deploys a very generous helping of analogy. For the preamble describes the Indigenous people of this continent as possessing particular "insights" into God's ways by virtue of God's sustained and sustaining work of "love and grace." Indigenous law, custom, and ceremony are seen positively as a reservoir of genuine truth enabled by the Spirit.[12] It is therefore quite difficult to see how such a positive and affirming evaluation of Indigenous knowledge could possibly be related to the condemnatory language of the apostle towards Greeks and barbarians, references to an idolatrous spirituality of animals, birds, and reptiles notwithstanding. This reader must conclude, therefore, that the enabling theology for the preamble must lie elsewhere, perhaps in some kind of colonial Christology. I'll return to a more positive version of that possibility at the end of the chapter.

The last characters I want to draw attention to from the story in the preamble are the "uniting churches." Note that these are not the Uniting Church. While the Uniting Church came into being in 1977, the uniting churches are the predecessor denominations that came together to form the Uniting Church. When they came to "Australia," they did so "as part

---

12. Uniting Church in Australia, *Basis of Union*, 41.

of the colonization process."[13] The colonizing churches, we are told, contained two groups with rather different attitudes towards First Peoples. Some approached Indigenous people with good intentions and a concern for solidarity and justice, appreciating and respecting Indigenous cultures and languages even as they proclaimed "the reconciling purpose of the Triune God found in the good news about Jesus Christ." Others, however, shared in the colonial practices of paternalism and racism towards First Peoples and were therefore complicit in dispossessing First Peoples of their land, language, culture, and spirituality. According to the story told in the preamble, it was this latter group that was strongest in the determination of church policy, for the uniting churches were "largely silent" as the dominant culture of Australia constructed a history of denial regarding both Aboriginal practices and the injustices inflicted on Indigenous peoples. This silence, according to the preamble, damaged both existing relationships with Indigenous peoples and the "integrity" of the gospel itself.[14]

By contrast, the Uniting Church formed after 1977 only did good things. It "took up" the cause of Indigenous peoples who challenged the status quo; it "discovered God's call . . . and entered into an ever deepening covenantal relationship with the Uniting Aboriginal and Islander Christian Congress."[15] The difference is profound in the way the story is told. The uniting churches were mostly bad. The Uniting Church is overwhelmingly good. There is more than just a hint, here, of what might be called ecclesiastical Darwinism.

In reality, of course, the Uniting Church has a long way to go when it comes to positive relations with Indigenous peoples, even the dwindling few who belong to its own congregations. One need search no further than the response of the Reverend Bill Hollingsworth, chairperson of the Uniting Aboriginal and Islander Christian Congress, at the decision of the Uniting Church Assembly in 1994 to join the UAICC in a "covenant." Having heard the president of the Uniting Church, Dr. Jill Tabart, offer an apology for many of the actions and inactions of the uniting churches with respect to First Peoples, Mr. Hollingsworth said:

> The UAICC believes that it is just for the Uniting Church . . . to
> offer a practical response to the past history of dispossession . . . by
> taking action to empower the UAICC ministry by offering to share

13. Uniting Church in Australia, *Basis of Union*, 40.
14. Uniting Church in Australia, *Basis of Union*, 41.
15. Uniting Church in Australia, *Basis of Union*, 41, 42.

the assets of the Uniting Church . . . Therefore it would be wrong to just say "I forgive," without reaching a commitment to work together to lay a new foundation upon which we may build a more just future together by ensuring that the Uniting Church plays an active role in providing adequate resources to address the present disadvantages caused by the past injustices . . . Your commitment to be practical will be assessed by your decisions to resource the Congress ministry and to be actively involved in ministry alongside and with Aboriginal and Islander people to change the present disadvantage.[16]

Having read through the reports of Congress to the Assembly since 1994, whilst some issues have been recently resolved with the Uniting Church (especially with regard to matters of governance and a degree of self-determination) the Congress still struggles to resource its ministries and regularly feels that the church really doesn't care about Aboriginal and Islander peoples. It is difficult to see how this situation might change any time soon.

Those last few words provide the means for a segue into the preamble's dealings with time. The preamble represents a standard euro-Christian approach to how time operates. It is historical and linear. It begins in the past, with the arrival in "Australia" of colonists, including the uniting churches. It follows the progress of that colonization and notes, with a degree of lament, the damage colonization did to cultures and spiritualities that were here "before" the arrival of the colonists. It then proceeds to enter a more recent time of friendly and supportive attitudes towards First Peoples in society and church and ends with the promise of a future in which First and Second peoples may live together harmoniously. There is a sense, here, that the future is already present simply by knowing or referring to a future. For the future is present through a promise. That is why the Uniting Church celebrates its 1994 covenant with the UAICC as a "foretaste of that coming reconciliation and renewal which is the end in view for the whole creation."[17] This sentence reproduces the character of eschatological time as it is represented in the *Basis of Union*:

> . . . the Church of God is committed to serve the world for which Christ died . . . and awaits with hope the day of the Lord Jesus Christ on which it will be clear that the kingdom of this world has

16. Uniting Church in Australia, *Basis of Union*, 37.

17. Uniting Church in Australia, *Basis of Union*, 42.

become the Kingdom of our Lord and of his Christ, and he shall reign for ever.[18]

The church lives between the time of Christ's death and resurrection and the final consummation of all things that he will bring; she is a pilgrim people, always on the way towards a promised goal; here she does not have a continuing city but seeks one to come.[19]

This euro-Christian concept of time, so omnipresent in the storytelling of what Derrida calls our "globalatinized," colonized world,[20] may be contrasted with Indigenous concepts of time which tend towards a complete disinterest in the distinctions between the past, the present, and the future. The dreaming stories associated with particular places on this continent, for example, work more with categories of space than of time. The sense, when these stories are told by Indigenous people rather than colonizers, is that the dreaming events are always happening, are always in motion, are always accessible. They are always about what is happening here and now. They are populated with characters that are alive now, forever permeating both landscape and relationships as they enfold and incorporate one another in an eternal present.[21]

This means, of course, that there are profound and persevering differences between the ways that many Indigenous people and colonizers experience reality. And this is true even amongst the most Westernized of our mobs. I am happiest and most carefree, for example, when I experience what the neuropsychologists call "flow,"[22] a sense that I am in a slip stream or eddy of meaningful activity in which the passage of time from a past toward a future is simply gone from either consciousness or concern. Meaningful activity, for me, can simply be walking through landscape or swimming through waterway, especially in my own country; or it can mean whiling away the day in conversation and the telling of stories. In both instances, the passage of time ceases to be meaningful as a determinative horizon.

18. Uniting Church in Australia, *Basis of Union*, 9.

19. Uniting Church in Australia, *Basis of Union*, 10.

20. Jacque Derrida's term for the alliance between Christianity and Anglo-American culture in its global influence. See Derrida, *Acts of Religion*, 67.

21. A recent volume which confirms this analysis is McGrath et al., *Everywhen*.

22. See, for example, the pioneering work of Nakamura and Csikszentmihályi, "Flow Theory," 195–206.

It also means that Indigenous people often struggle to understand why there must be such a gaping temporal gap in the time between *knowing* that something is good and wise and *making* it happen. Why must we wait? If it is good and wise, it should be happening right now, should it not? And that good and wise thing should keep happening, should it not? Why should it stop happening, why should it disappear into a past? Many Aboriginal and Torres Strait Islander people find it difficult to understand the delays the wider Uniting Church seems happy to keep in place when it comes to the doing of justice. If you agree that justice is good and wise, why is the arrival of that justice substituted with a promise, effectively a stand-in for justice while justice is not here? To us, such deferrals confirm that it is colonization that occupies the eternal present, not justice or the healing of country.

As I said in earlier chapters, the determining horizon for a great many Indigenous people is not in fact time, but space; or, even better, if we must use English, *place*. That is why our dreaming stories are all country specific. Each enumerates the relationship of certain creator ancestors with a particular place: hybrid beings made of country, of animal, and of human flesh, creator beings who continue to live within that place to instruct its appointed caretakers with the wisdom they need to sustain life in that place. We have our own names for these places, repeated in ceremony, songlines, and other forms of ritual storytelling. We have names for every landscape and waterway on the continent. The names refer to stories, and the stories teach us both who we are and what we are to do. Country, for us, becomes something of a sacred text in which we might "read" the wisdom we need to live peacefully, sustainably, and well in the places we are given. Jews have their Torah, Christians their Bible, but we have country to show us the way.

The preamble of the Uniting Church's constitution also reproduces a typology of place. It is a colonial typology, a possessive typology, which has grown not from the soil or waterways beneath our feet or the cosmic energies of the creator ancestors who are our progenitors and kin, but from the minds and actions of those who arrived here recently from over the seas, those whom the preamble calls, in another act of historical erasure, "Second Peoples."[23] Let's begin with the way in which these lands and waterways are named. They are named not with the stories of our ancestors, but with the story of invasion and colonization: Australia. For make no

23. "Second Peoples" as a phrase creates the illusion of some kind of analogical equivalence between the manner in which Indigenous people and settlers come to be in the land, thus erasing the infinite qualitative difference between an Indigenous belonging *to* country and the violence inherent in colonial annexation *of* country.

mistake, "Australia" is a name for stealing, murder, rape, and violence. Even its origin in the latin *terra australis* bears witness to this. To speak of a "land to the south" you have to imagine that where you stand, in the north, is the prime meridian, the center of the world. "Australia" therefore stands for the violence put into play when a European imagination imposes itself, by force and without negotiation or treaty, on these lands that we call nipaluna (Hobart) or Naarm (Melbourne) or Meeanjin (Brisbane).

A second way in which the preamble writes this colonial spatiality is by locating the Triune God of the Uniting Church and, indeed, of the church catholic right here, with First Peoples, before the colonists even arrived. The advance party for colonization, according to this logic, was the Christian God. Allow me to remind you what the preamble says:

> The First Peoples had already encountered the Creator God before the arrival of the colonisers; the Spirit was already in the land revealing God to the people through law, custom and ceremony. The same love and grace that was finally and fully revealed in Jesus Christ sustained the First Peoples and gave them particular insights into God's ways.[24]

Now let me say this as delicately as I can. This theological substitution of the Triune God of Christians—here named "Creator," "Spirit," and "Jesus Christ"—for our creator ancestors, is as pure an act of colonial erasure as I have seen. And it is immediately repeated when the preamble claims that our law, our custom, and our ceremony teach us not about country, and how to live in it wisely, but rather about the "love and grace that was finally and fully revealed in Jesus Christ." This kind of substitution is a centering of the white possessive in its most paradigmatic form: the overwriting of an Indigenous cosmic imaginary with the cosmic imaginary of an invading and totalizing force. In this instance, by a colonizing Christian church. The moral problem here is a fundamental lack of humility before the continuing mystery of another land, another people, another way of construing the world.

Unfortunately, by telling this story in history-like language, readers of the preamble are encouraged to take what is being said as matter-of-fact prose. There is no obvious deployment here of a poetics of analogy or metaphor. Analogy, a comparison of two different realities in which certain family resemblances might be discerned, could have been quite helpful at this point. It would have communicated the possibility that this settler Christian

---

24. Uniting Church in Australia, *Basis of Union*, 41.

theological language is, at most, provisional and partial in its claim that there is a relationship between Christian and Indigenous cosmologies. If the preamble had said something like, "First Nations people see the world as A and our church sees the world as B. A and B are obviously very different. Still, isn't it interesting that some elements of A and some elements of B look, sound, and smell quite similar? Perhaps there are grounds here for the beginnings of a mutually enriching conversation?"—that, I think would have been much better.

I submit that there is not only poetry in the deployment of metaphorical language, but also humility, wondering, and a deep sense of respect for mystery. Who amongst us has not been transformed by an encounter with mystery? If we encounter the genuinely other, as other—not merely as a vessel into which we presume to pour whatever we think we know already—then we expose ourselves to the possibility of genuine surprise, of learning, even of laughter. We may, through an act of basic respect and humility, experience that parabolic twist in our perspective by which what is apparently familiar becomes unfamiliar and strange. And that, I propose, is the beginning of every adventure worth having. Now, whilst I am certain that the authors of the preamble had the very best of intentions, their actual words simply substitute a colonial story about the supremacy of Christ for an Indigenous story about country. In this way, they accomplish precisely the opposite of their intentions for good: they rob First Peoples of the depth, height, and breadth of our spirituality.

RESTARTING THE CONVERSATION

Allow me to conclude by proposing a modest (and hardly original) way of restarting the conversation between First Peoples and colonial Christianity on a more respectful footing. If Christian settlers were to engage in the conversation by first listening, listening deeply, to what Indigenous people are saying about country, I think they would learn some very interesting things.

They would learn that:

> We are all born from the watery womb of country;
> country feeds us with the pure nectar of her own life;
> from the beginning of creation, and in every moment, country dies;
> by her death, everything that is dead is made alive;
> country teaches us who we are, and how we are to live;

country is our mother, our father, our uncle and aunty, our sister
and our brother;
country is our kin, and in her familial body we find that all creation—plants, animals, even the stary host above—are kin to us
as well;
country teaches us to care for our kin as country cares for us;
country bids us to imitate what we see in country—to watch, to
listen, to imbibe and to notice—to take what we learn into ourselves and write it on our hearts;
and when we die, country takes us into the heart of her own death
so that we may be born to an intimacy that is more wonderful than
anything we could think or imagine.[25]

And perhaps, by listening and learning so, the church might learn that
all that Indigenous people say about country is also said of Christ in the
Scriptures, he in whom "all things in heaven and on earth were created,
things visible and invisible" (Col 1:15b). Perhaps the church might then
begin to see that Indigenous people are not only the First Peoples of this
land, but also the first theologians, the first thinkers of the divine life in
this place. Perhaps, then, the church might consent to submit itself to the
disciplines of an Indigenous imagination and an Indigenous way of life and
so think the meaning of the Christ within the imaginative container of *this*
country, rather than that of Europe or the Middle East.

These reflections leave a lot of questions unanswered, of course. How
is it that a tradition that habitually centers the particularity of Israel, and of
Israel's Jesus, is compatible with a tradition that might think of Jesus as a
creator ancestor who is by no means the first or the most preeminent? How
might a tradition that thinks from the earth, from the complex communion
we call "country," be compatible with a tradition that privileges the human,
and Jesus as a particular human, as the center of all reality? I have sought
to address some of those questions in this book. But as I get older, I tend to
leave many of these questions permanently open. With Rilke, I feel intui-
tively that it is in the living of the questions through our search for intimacy
and belonging, that many of our most tangled dilemmas are resolved.[26]
Whilst many theologians would still like to tidy up, and therefore master or
control, the radical undecidability of many of our enduring questions, I do
not. I prefer to let stories and traditions sit side by side like acquaintances

25. The discerning reader will notice that this is a slightly different version of the
poem I shared in chapter 3.

26. See the fourth letter in Rilke, *Letters.*

around that campfire I talked about in the introduction to this volume. If we sit there long enough, if we return to each other at the campfire again and again, if we listen carefully to the songs that are most close and dear and sing them out of the depths of our vulnerability, we might find that we love each other: not despite the polyvalence of our songs, but because of that polyvalence.

CHAPTER 12

The Kenosis Model

How the Churches Can Deal with Their Colonial Legacy[1]

The churches of Australia have a colonial legacy. To summarize something of what I've said already in this book: the churches participated in, and still benefit from, the stealing of our lands; the churches participated in the massacres, the frontier conflicts and the genocidal policies concerning our people because the people who committed these atrocities were overwhelmingly Christian; the churches took the lead in the attempted destruction of our spiritual way of life, especially during the missions period; the churches participated in, and remain mostly silent in the face of, the ecocide which accompanied the genocide.

Many Australian churches continue to deploy an imaginative *terra nullius* regarding our people by effectively pretending that we don't exist. Our voices are not there in the policymaking bodies of their councils, their mission agencies, and their educational institutions. Such churches are uncurious about the country we walk on and the knowledge we have of its ways and its spirit. There continues to be a lack of active interest in our theology which, as I hope this book has demonstrated, is different to settler theology in fundamental ways.

This brief account gives rise to a fundamental question: How are the churches to reckon with this colonial heritage? Well, to answer this, I will

---

1. An earlier version of the paper was posted on the ABC's Religion and Ethics website. Deverell, "For Your Sakes."

appeal to the Pauline tradition as we have it in the New Testament: first in the Christological hymn of Philippians 2 and then in the exhortation towards an equitable distribution of resources in 2 Corinthians 8.

Philippians 2 says, in part:

> If then there is any encouragement in Christ, any consolation from love, any sharing in the Spirit, any compassion and sympathy, make my joy complete: be of the same mind, having the same love, being in full accord and of one mind. Do nothing from selfish ambition or conceit, but in humility regard others as better than yourselves. Let each of you look not to your own interests, but to the interests of others. Let the same mind be in you that was in Christ Jesus,
>
> who, though he was in the form of God,
> did not regard equality with God
> as something to be exploited,
> but emptied himself,
> taking the form of a slave,
> being born in human likeness.
> And being found in human form,
> he humbled himself
> and became obedient to the point of death—
> even death on a cross.
>
> Therefore God also highly exalted him
> and gave him the name
> that is above every name,
> so that at the name of Jesus
> every knee should bend,
> in heaven and on earth and under the earth,
> and every tongue should confess
> that Jesus Christ is Lord
> to the glory of God the Father.
> (Phil 2:1–11)

Now, I want you to notice three things about this passage. First, it is addressed to a congregation of Christians who are divided, one against another, who are selfish because individuals look out for their own survival and wellbeing at the expense of others. Second, the apostle contrasts this behavior to that of Jesus who, though enjoying a certain ascendency in the cosmic order of things, empties himself (*kenosis*) of all such power and privilege to come amongst human beings as a slave (*doulos*) who has no power at all. Finally, the passage creates a model, a pathway, which Christian communities are encouraged to imitate and follow to be truly alive and vital. It is the path of *kenosis*: a dying to self-aggrandizement and a rising to a rather more other-centered mode of being. A dying to all that is power-over, power-acquisitive, power-for self-alone, and a rising to power-with, power-giving, power for the wellbeing of others.

But now to the key question that confronts us in the colony of Australia. How are settler Christians—they who have empowered and enriched themselves at the expense of Indigenous people—going to let that power go? How are they to redress the imbalance? How will they take the power acquired through genocide and ecocide and return it to those they wronged, and continue to wrong? For Christians, I would contend, it can never be a question of *whether* such power is returned. It can only be a question of *how*. For if settler Christians do not imitate Christ in this manner, how can they really be called Christians at all?

So, let's turn to a bit of that "how," beginning with a paragraph from 2 Corinthians 8:

> For you know the generous act of our Lord Jesus Christ, that though he was rich, yet for your sakes he became poor, so that by his poverty you might become rich. And in this matter I am giving my advice: it is appropriate for you who began last year not only to do something but even to desire to do something— now finish doing it, so that your eagerness may be matched by completing it according to your means. For if the eagerness is there, the gift is acceptable according to what one has—not according to what one does not have. I do not mean that there should be relief for others and pressure on you, but it is a question of a fair balance between your present abundance and their need, so that their abundance may be for your need, in order that there may be a fair balance. As it is written,
>
> "The one who had much did not have too much,
> and the one who had little did not have too little." (2 Cor 8:9–15)

The context here is that there are two church communities, one that is very poor and another that is quite wealthy. And we're talking actual, economic, resources here, not so-called "spiritual" resources, intangible things like wisdom or humility. We're talking money and property. The apostle appeals to the rich church to share its abundant resources with the poor church by invoking, again, that kenotic Christology. The argument, in summary, goes something like this: "Remember the story of Jesus. He was rich, but he became poor for your sakes, and he did that so that you might acquire some of his riches. So, like Jesus, I'd like you to hand over your wealth, your money, to the poor church. I'd like you to act with the same love, the same generosity of spirit, as that you found in Christ. Not, mind you, to the point where you become destitute and in need of help yourselves. Think, rather, that the excess you enjoy can provide what is lacking in the poorer community." This is St. Paul's "Christian socialism." The goal here is something like a balance, an equality, so that both communities have what they need.

Now, obviously, there is no hint in this text that the rich church gained its riches by stealing its wealth from the poor church. But this being so, how much more ought the colonial church consider the ways in which it might return its stolen resources to First Nations communities from whom it was stolen? Now, usually when I start to say these kinds of things the question that arises, right away, is "Okay, but what would that actually look like for our own local church community, or our own denominational organization?" The answer might become the substance of treaty proposals, ways in which the deeply uneven balance of power between colonial and Indigenous communities might be rendered more equal. So, I encourage the members of settler churches to consider the following practical proposals.

At the denominational level, plan to hand the properties you were given by the Crown without fee or compensation back to their original Aboriginal owners, also without fee or compensation. Where properties were purchased from the Crown, or else from subsequent owners, arrange to vest the title of those properties in the name of the original Indigenous owners under a leaseback scheme. This makes both the use, or the disposal, of those properties a matter of negotiation and careful treaty between Indigenous people and settlers. Where purchased properties remain in the hands of the denomination because local mob do not want to become owners, contribute half of the commercial income on such properties to mob: 25 percent to local owners and 25 percent to Indigenous ministries run by and for our people. The same would apply when properties are sold—split the proceeds of the sale.

At the local congregational level, contribute 10 percent of your annual budget to ministries run by Aboriginal or Torres Strait Islander people, for Aboriginal or Torres Strait Islander people, in perpetuity. Whether there is an existing denominational agreement for the leaseback of properties in place or not, approach your local mob with the question: Could we form a relationship with you that includes your use of this space for community gatherings and programs, without fee or compensation?

A more just sharing of the land churches have stolen from us, including its commercial value, would obviously make a huge difference to the kinds of programs Aboriginal Controlled Community Organizations could run to assist our people to escape from poverty and reclaim our rightful heritage as the sovereign peoples of this country. It would also make a huge difference to our capacity to reclaim and pass on our practical wisdom and spirituality to the next generation, whether Indigenous or settler. In the church, the sharing of these resources would provide a sure and reliable economic base for the work of our Aboriginal and Torres Strait Islander ministries, and for our theological research and teaching. The fruit of these ministries would make for stronger Aboriginal and Torres Strait Islander communities and a higher profile for our spiritualities and theologies in the knowledge repositories of our nation, knowledges that are desperately needed if we are to heal and form a more mutually supportive relationship with country.

But let's be clear. Land and resource justice is just a beginning, a foundation. At the same time, the churches would do well to allow us to set up camp in the center of their corporate life: to allow us to migrate from the darkness at the edge of town—where we are out of sight, out of earshot, out of mind and heart—into the places where theology is formulated, and decisions made about ministry and mission. For they need us. Historic settler churches are in decline because they are seen as either too out of touch or too corrupt to make a meaningful contribution to solving the many problems that plague us as a Commonwealth or as a planet. Aboriginal knowledges, on the other hand, are on the up. Universities are including our wisdom about the earth, the stars, flora, and fauna, as well as the human body and mind, in their curricula. Climatologists, botanists, and environmental scientists are consulting with us about how to better manage country. Fire authorities are seeking to learn about our fire-farming techniques. The churches need to get with the program! They need us to help them deploy their theological and ministry resources in ways that help and do not harm, in ways that produce patterns of healing and care rather than wounding and indifference. The churches need us. So why are we not on their councils, boards, and ministry teams? Why are we not amongst their bishops, their general secretaries, and moderators? Why are we not amongst their theological teachers and researchers?

For our theology is rather different to that of settler churches. To summarize the argument of this book, our theology is centered in:

- the community of creation, rather than the community of human beings alone

- the ancestral divinity of country, rather than divinity of Jesus alone

- the ethics of caring for country, rather than the ethics of caring for human beings alone

- the governance of people by country (learning to imitate the patterns and processes of the non-human world), rather than the governance of country by people

- the mission of country together with human community, rather than the mission of Christians alone

- rituals which celebrate and make present the ancestral divinity of country, rather than the rituals of Christian Europe alone.

Our First Peoples theology, in fact, is much older than that of the Christian churches, up to a hundred thousand years older. It is also deeply connected to how we live sustainably and well within this country. If settler theology is to ever leave the shores of the European Enlightenment and come to live in this place, some radical transformations need to take place. We can help the churches to make those transformations. To be frank, the settler churches don't know what they don't know, and what they think they know is proving quite inadequate in the face of the damage they've done since they arrived here. We can help with that.

So, let me be so bold as to suggest that the churches are at a *"kairos"* threshold of decision: a timely, critical, or opportune moment. They are at a crossroads. The churches can either continue upon the path they have taken since they arrived here, the colonizing path, which is to make themselves the center of all things and therefore leading exploiters of both this land and its First Peoples. Or they can take a different path, a path which would mean decentering themselves, giving up that power and status they have become accustomed to, and listening, instead, to the wisdom of country and its children. The prophet Jeremiah might have said something similar. I conclude by citing chapter 6, verse 16:

Thus says the Lord:
Stand at the crossroads, and look,
ask for the ancient paths,
ask where the good way lies;
and walk in it.
Then you will find rest for your souls.

Perhaps the churches might now answer the divine voice differently than did the ancient kingdom of Judah? I quote again:

But they said, "We will not walk in it."

"The Last Will Be First"

Middle-Class Values and Aboriginal Disadvantage

On Easter Monday, 1996, at the famous Stawell Gift Athletics Carnival, an extraordinary running race was held. It was the four hundred metres handicap race for women. Now, for those of you who are unfamiliar with the language of athletics, the word "handicap" does not here refer to a race for people with an identified disability. It refers, instead, to the practice of spacing the runners out as the race begins so that the ones with the strongest pre-race record start at "scratch," that is, the starting line, and the other, weaker runners are given a variety of head starts further along the course. In theory, this means that were everyone to run their personal best times, they would all finish with a dead heat at the finish line. On this particular occasion, one runner, Catherine Astrid Salome Freeman—a sixteen-year-old Kuku Yalanji girl from Woorabinda in Queensland—was the only runner to start at scratch, and the next closest runner was placed a full fifty-four metres ahead of her as the race began. Some old and grainy footage of that race is worth a look. For it shows the young Cathy Freeman not only catching the field of white runners ahead of her, but also enduring a big shove from one of them as the field passes the 350-metre mark. Amazingly, Cathy keeps her form and comes home to win the event by a whisker.[1]

That Cathy won and went on to become both a world and Olympic champion in this same event, is something of a modern miracle. For she is Aboriginal. She belongs to a people whose lands and waterways were stolen

---

1. Jump Media and Marketing, "1996."

at the point of a gun, whose ancestors were massacred, poisoned, raped, shackled, removed from country and kin, enslaved in missions, orphanages, and individual homes as domestic servants, and now continue to be the single most disadvantaged ethnic group in the Australian Commonwealth on any measure. Aboriginal people are twice as likely to be living with a disability, four times more likely to live with a chronic disease, twice as likely to take our own lives, and thirty-seven times more likely to be imprisoned than any other Australian. Aboriginal people are one thousand times more likely to die in police custody.[2] On that Easter Monday in 1996 Cathy was at the back of the line on handicapping. But she was also at the back of the line when it came to the likelihood that she would even be there to compete. That she was able to slip past every single white runner, including the one who tried to take her out of the race with a physical shove, is simply amazing. From last in the race to first. From last in this country to sporting royalty.

There is a story in Matthew's Gospel about the last becoming first:

> For the kingdom of heaven is like a landowner who went out early in the morning to hire laborers for his vineyard. After agreeing with the laborers for the usual daily wage, he sent them into his vineyard.
>
> When he went out about nine o'clock, he saw others standing idle in the marketplace; and he said to them, 'You also go into the vineyard, and I will pay you whatever is right.' So they went. When he went out again about noon and about three o'clock, he did the same. And about five o'clock he went out and found others standing around; and he said to them, 'Why are you standing here idle all day?' They said to him, 'Because no one has hired us.' He said to them, 'You also go into the vineyard.'
>
> When evening came, the owner of the vineyard said to his manager, 'Call the laborers and give them their pay, beginning with the last and then going to the first.' When those hired about five o'clock came, each of them received the usual daily wage. Now when the first came, they thought they would receive more; but each of them also received the usual daily wage. And when they received it, they grumbled against the landowner, saying, 'These last worked only one hour, and you have made them equal to us who have borne the burden of the day and the scorching heat.'

2. These statistics are extrapolated from Commonwealth Government data in the annual "Closing the Gap" report. Australian Government, "Closing the Gap."

> But he replied to one of them, 'Friend, I am doing you no
> wrong; did you not agree with me for the usual daily wage? Take
> what belongs to you and go; I choose to give to this last the same
> as I give to you. Am I not allowed to do what I choose with what
> belongs to me? Or are you envious because I am generous?' So the
> last will be first, and the first will be last (Matt 20:1–16)

In this, one of Jesus's most intriguing parables, he says that the kingdom of heaven is like a landowner who has a vineyard. The landowner goes out at dawn to the marketplace in town where willing laborers are most likely to gather. He hires those who are there after agreeing to pay them the usual daily wage, a denarius, and they head over the vineyard to pick grapes. But there are not enough laborers to secure the harvest, so the landowner goes out again at nine, twelve, three, and five to hire more workers. Each are hired on the promise that they will be paid "what is right" for their time.

Now, at knock off time, each of the workers are indeed paid, beginning with the last hired, and finishing with the first. Those hired at the beginning of the day are incensed to learn that all the other workers, even those hired at five o'clock in the afternoon, are to be paid the full daily wage, just as they are. They complain bitterly about these late comers "being made equal" to themselves, even though they have worked longer. But the landowner responds, "Did you not agree to work for a denarius? That is what you have been paid. Are you calling me evil because I am generous towards these others?" After the storytelling is complete, Jesus then summarizes its main message for his hearers: "the last will be first and the first will be last."

Now, I've used this story in Bible studies across twenty-seven years of public ministry, and I can report that almost every white, middle-class person who hears the story for the first time responds, like clockwork, "But that is so unfair!" That experience has convinced me that most settlers tend to identify most strongly with the people hired at the beginning of the day. Why? Because they are raised from birth to believe that if you don't work, you don't eat, and that justice is primarily about getting what you deserve because of your hard work. If you work hard, you rightly expect to be rewarded in proportion to the amount of work you have done. Since justice is proportional, it follows that those who work less than you should be paid less than you. Now, if that is what you believe, if life is most properly a meritocracy in which the hardest workers take the lion's share of the rewards, then the behavior of the landowner in our parable is guaranteed to offend. For it strikes at the very heart of this white, middle-class work ethic.

It questions, and possibly even mocks, that ethic's certainties about what is fair and what is just.

Of course, if you are white and middle-class, there are probably a lot of things that you cannot see. You may not be aware, for example, that you have a disability, an ailment that I have named "white-blindness."[3] White-blindness is an incapacity to see what life might be like for people who are not white and middle-class, for people whose very different social location may teach them quite different lessons about the world and how it works. When I, a trawloolway man, read this parable, I identify not with the people who were hired at the beginning of the day, but with those who were hired at five o'clock. For I know, deep in my marrow, that those who are ready to work at six o'clock in the morning enjoy a long list of advantages that I simply cannot count on. They, for example, are most likely able-bodied, which gives them a significant advantage when it comes to being job ready. The fact that they are ready to work at six o'clock in the morning means that they also enjoy good mental health. I, on the other hand, do not. Generations of racism from the most powerful towards my people means that I carry with me a weight that is very, very difficult to slough off. It is difficult to get up each day with a certainty that I will be treated fairly when multiple generations before me were not. And that has been confirmed, many hundreds of times over, in my own experience. Simply by being Aboriginal, I am three times more likely to regularly experience high levels of psychological distress than other Australians, and that makes getting out of bed in the morning quite difficult, sometimes. I won't go on, but I hope you are getting the picture.

From a sociocontextual point of view, it is clear that those who are more latterly hired by the landowner are very likely to have been the most marginalized members of Judean society at the time: landless peasants who are continually exhausted because most landowners exploit their labor for a pittance; widows or "unclean" women who have no male patriarch to protect them; indigenous people like the Canaanite women we encounter in chapter 15 of the gospel, the one whose daughter was tormented by a demon, a demon some scholars happily name "colonization." And so on. These people are late to the marketplace because they have learned—through cold, hard, experience—that there is little to be gained by being there early. They are outcasts, they are rarely picked for the work available, and therefore there is little point in turning up at all.

3. See Deverell, *Gondwana*, 50.

If you read the parable from that point of view, then this story is not about the proportionality of justice, as white middle-class expectation might have it. It is not even about a failure of such justice. It is about grace, here defined as an excess of loving generosity toward the last and the least. To all who believe that justice is satisfied by getting what you deserve, this might come as very bad news indeed! Because if you believe in meritocracy, grace proclaims the very opposite: that it is the last and the least, those who are least deserving in the eyes of the meritocracy, who can expect to receive the love and mercy of the creator and landowner of all the earth.

For most people who live on this planet, those who are not white and middle-class, the grace at the heart of the parable is the very best of news. For it tells us that while the world run by white people may have forgotten us, if it even acknowledges our existence at all, God has not forgotten us. From the lips of Jesus, the very son of God, we learn that God will take us from our customary place at the very back of the field, and help us along, with Cathy, to the winner's podium. The last, those who get barely enough work to get by, will nevertheless be made equal with those who can depend on work every day.

Let's be clear, however, that none of this happens by magic. Faith will not, for example, immediately deliver the poor and the oppressed to the front of the queue. Faith, rather, will assure the poor one, the enslaved one, that she or he is loved, accepted and free in Christ. And this knowledge, in turn, will give her the confidence and courage to have a go, and keep having a go, even if the chips are down and the system is against you.

When Cathy won her gold medal at the Sydney Olympics in the year 2000 she had some help. She said that her ancestors rose from the ground beneath her feet to fill her with the strength and confidence she needed to prevail against the odds. Here Cathy is speaking in an Aboriginal way about the divine. For us, the divine is at work in our ancestors, who inhabit the earth and flora and fauna, all about us, just as the Holy Spirit lived in Christ and now lives in his church. Cathy is saying, therefore, that the confidence and help of her ancestors filled her with everything she needed to run, and to run without giving up. The ancestors do not run the race for us. They give us the power and courage, rather, to finish the race as equal partners with all who have had a better start in life.

For, in the end, it is grace that saves us all, through faith, whether we are at the bottom of the social pile, or in the middle, or at the top. It is not our work, nor our status, as the most powerful would measure it. Such is the way of our ancestors. Such is the way of Christ. Such is the way of the gospel. So, in the wake of this reading of Jesus' parable, I leave you with just two simple challenges. If you are poor, God in Christ has come to raise you up, so trust that his grace will get you there, even to the banqueting halls of "heaven," however you might understand that. If you are wealthy, then God would have you leave those chains behind for the sake of the poorest and least. For by emptying yourselves of such riches (as Christ did) and sharing your wealth with the least (as Christ did) you will become rich in the eyes of God.

Bibliography

Abbatangelo, Ben. "Apocalypse and the Indigenous Imagination." *IndigenousX*, April 5, 2023. https://indigenousx.com.au/indigenous-imagination.

AEF. "Welcome to the Aboriginal Evangelical Fellowship of Aus. Inc." AEF, 2023. https://aef.org.au/.

AIATSIS. "The 1967 Referendum." https://aiatsis.gov.au/explore/1967-referendum.

———. "The Mabo Case." https://aiatsis.gov.au/explore/mabo-case.

Anthony, Thalia. "Criminal Justice and Transgression on Northern Australian Cattle Stations." In *Transgressions: Critical Australian Indigenous Histories*, edited by Ingereth Macfarlane and Mark Hannah, 35–61. Canberra, ACT: Australian National University Press, 2007.

———. "FactCheck: Are First Australians the Most Imprisoned People on Earth?" *The Conversation*, June 6, 2017. https://theconversation.com/factcheck-are-first-australians-the-most-imprisoned-people-on-earth-78528.

Australian Government Productivity Commission. "Closing the Gap Information Repository." https://www.pc.gov.au/closing-the-gap-data.

Australian Human Rights Commission. "Past Projects." https://humanrights.gov.au/about/get-involved/events/national-sorry-day.

Barthes, Roland. "Death of the Author." In *Image, Music, Text*. Translated by Stephen Heath. London, UK: Fontana, 1977.

Berndt, Ronald N., and Catherine H. Berndt. *End of an Era: Aboriginal Labour in the Northern Territory*. Canberra: Australian Institute of Aboriginal Studies, 1987.

Boyce, James. *1835: The Founding of Melbourne and the Conquest of Australia*. Collingwood, Victoria: Black Inc., 2012.

———. *God's Own Country? The Anglican Church and Tasmanian Aborigines*. Hobart, Tasmania: Anglicare Tasmania, 2001.

———. *Van Diemen's Land*. Collingwood, Victoria: Black Inc., 2008.

Brett, Mark G. *Locations of God: Political Theology in the Hebrew Bible*. Oxford, UK: Oxford University Press, 2019.

Brown, Tina. *The Palace Papers: Inside the House of Windsor—The Truth and the Turmoil*. Melbourne, Victoria: Penguin, 2022.

Bunjilaka Aboriginal Cultural Centre. "Eastern Kulin Seasonal Calendar." Museums Victoria, 2023. https://museumsvictoria.com.au/bunjilaka/about-us/eastern-kulin-seasonal-calendar/.

Caputo, John D. *Demythologizing Heidegger*. Bloomington, IN: Indiana University Press, 1993.

Champion, Denise. *Anaditj*. Edited by Rosemary Derwerse. Port Augusta, SA: Denise Champion, 2021.

Curthoys, Ann. "Expulsion, Exodus and Exile in White Australian Historical Mythology." *Journal of Australian Studies* 23 (1999) 1–19.

Curthoys, Ann, and Jessie Mitchell. *Taking Liberty: Indigenous Rights and Settler Self-Government in Colonial Australia, 1830–1890*. New York: Cambridge University Press, 2020.

Derrida, Jacques. *Acts of Religion*. Edited by Gil Anidjar. New York & London: Routledge, 2002.

———. *Of Grammatology*. Translated by Gayatri Chakravorty Spivak. Baltimore, MD: John Hopkins University Press, 1997.

Desert Fathers. *The Sayings of the Desert Fathers: The Alphabetical Collection*. Translated by Benedicta Ward. London and Oxford, UK: Cistercian, 1984.

Dudgeon, Pat, and Tanja Hirvonen. "Why Are We Losing So Many Indigenous Children to Suicide?" *The Conversation*, March 29, 2019. https://theconversation.com/why-are-we-losing-so-many-indigenous-children-to-suicide-114284.

Deverell, Garry J. *The Bonds of Freedom: Vows, Sacraments and the Formation of the Christian Self*. Eugene, OR: Wipf & Stock, 2008.

Deverell, Garry Worete. "Bushfires and Colonial Mismanagement of Aboriginal Land." *NAIITS* 17 (2019) 176–79.

———. "Garry's Speech to the Anglican Diocese of Melbourne's Synod in Oct 2019." https://uncommonprayers.blogspot.com/2019/10/garrys-speech-to-anglican-diocese-of.html.

———. *Gondwana Theology: A Trawloolway Man Reflects upon Christian Faith*. Reservoir, Victoria: Morning Star, 2018.

———. "Homily." Koonung Uniting Church, Lent 2022. https://youtu.be/8ol2ahPgOAM.

______. "Next Steps for Reconciliation." http://christologia.net/deverell_motion_synod2019.pdf.

———. "Our Vision for Indigenous Studies at the University of Divinity." *Australian Journal of Mission Studies* 1 (2021) 20–23.

———. "'For Your Sakes He Became Poor . . .': How the Churches Can Reckon with Their Colonial Legacy." ABC Religion and Ethics, October 23, 2022. https://www.abc.net.au/religion/churches-and-their-colonial-legacy-garry-deverell/14091754.

Deverell, Garry, and Naomi Wolfe. "Protocol for Welcome to/Acknowledgment of Country." https://divinity.edu.au/documents/protocol-for-welcome-to-acknowledgement-of-country.

Eliot, T. S. *Four Quartets*. London, UK: Faber, 2019.

Ecological Society of Australia. "Australia's Species Extinction Crisis in Numbers: 2019." https://www.ecolsoc.org.au/?hottopic-entry=australias-species-extinction-crisis-in-numbers-2019.

Evans, Jennifer. "Giving Voice to the Sacred Black Female Body in Takayna Country." In *Indigenous Perspectives on Sacred Natural Sites: Culture, Governance and Conservation*, edited by Jonathan Lijeblad and Bas Verschuuren, 15–31. London, UK: Routledge, 2019.

Finlay, Grant. *Good People Always Crackney in Heaven: Mythic Conversations in Lutruwita/Tasmania*. Hobart, Tasmania: Fullers, 2019.

Forster, Dion A. "Post-Foundational Theology and the Contribution of African Approaches to Consciousness and Identity." *Verbum et Ecclesia* 2 (2021) 1–10.

Gamage, Bill. *The Biggest Estate on Earth: How Aborigines Made Australia*. Crows Nest, NSW: Allen and Unwin, 2012.

Gotev, Georgi. "In Putin's Words: Why Russia Invaded Ukraine." *Euroactiv*, February 24, 2022. https://www.euractiv.com/section/global-Europe/news/in-putins-words-why-russia-invaded-ukraine/.

Habel, Norm, et al. *De-colonising the Biblical Narrative Volume 2: A First Nations De-Colonising of Genesis 12–25*. Hindmarsh, SA: ATF, 2023.

Hackett, Erna Kim. "Why I Stopped Talking About Racial Reconciliation and Started Talking About White Supremacy." *Inheritance Magazine* 66 (2020). https://www.inheritfancemag.com/stories/why-i-stopped-talking-about-racial-reconciliation-and-started-talking-about-white-supremacy.

Harris, John. "Hiding the Bodies: The Myth of the Humane Colonisation of Aboriginal Australia." *Aboriginal History* 27 (2003) 79–104.

———. *One Blood: 200 years of Aboriginal Encounter with Christianity*. 3rd ed. Fullerton, SA: Concilia Ltd, 2018.

Hart, Kevin. *The Trespass of the Sign: Deconstruction, Theology, and Philosophy*. 2nd ed. New York: Fordham University Press, 2000.

Haskins, Victoria. "Sickness and Slavery: Reflecting upon Aboriginal Domestic Workers and Disease in Aboriginal History." *Labour History* 123 (2022) 15–20.

Heidegger, Martin. *Identity and Difference*. Translated by Joan Stambaugh. New York: Harper and Row, 1969.

Heng, Geraldine. *The Invention of Race in the European Middle Ages*. Cambridge, UK: Cambridge University Press, 2018.

Hitchens, Christopher. *The Monarchy: A Critique of Britain's Favourite Fetish*. London, UK: Vintage, 2012.

Howard-Brook, Wes. *"Come Out, My People!": God's Call Out of Empire in the Bible and Beyond*. Maryknoll, NY: Orbis, 2010.

Isles, Martin. "Welcome to Country: Is it Showing Respect or Affirming Paganism? The Truth of It Ep.100." https://youtu.be/BOJ5uNf_EaQ.

Jennings, Willi James. *The Christian Imagination: Theology and the Origins of Race*. New Haven, CT: Yale University Press, 2011.

Jump Media and Marketing. "1996 Australia Post Stawell Gift Cathy Freeman Women's 400m Final." Posted March 17, 2010, YouTube, https://youtu.be/DUQLV4gnWNY.

Kristeva, Julia. *Tales of Love*. Translated by Leon S. Roudiez. New York: Columbia University Press, 1987.

Lake, Meredith. *The Bible in Australia: A Cultural History*. Sydney, NSW: New South Publishing, 2020.

Lehman, Greg. "Regarding the Savages: Visual Representation of Tasmanian Aborigines in the 19th Century." PhD diss., University of Tasmania, 2017.

Madison, Sarah. *The Colonial Fantasy: Why White Australia Can't Solve Black Problems*. Crows Nest, NSW: Allen & Unwin, 2019.

Marion, Jean-Luc. *God Without Being: Hors-Texte*. Translated by Thomas A. Carlson. Chicago: University of Chicago Press, 1991.

———. *In Excess: Studies of Saturated Phenomena*. Translated by Robyn Horner and Vincent Berraud. New York: Fordham University Press, 2002.

———. *Prolegomena to Charity*. Translated by Stephen Lewis. New York: Fordham University Press, 2002.

McFague, Sallie. *The Body of God: An Ecological Theology*. Minneapolis, MN: Fortress, 1993.

McGrath, Anne, et al., eds. *Everywhen: Australia and the Language of Deep History*. Sydney, NSW: University of New South Wales Press, 2023.

Moltmann, Jürgen. *The Way of Jesus Christ: Christology in Messianic Dimensions*. Minneapolis, MN: Fortress, 1993.

Moreton-Robinson, Aileen. *Talkin' Up to the White Woman: Aboriginal Women and Feminism*. St Lucia, Queensland: University of Queensland Press, 2000.

———. *The White Possessive: Property, Power and Indigenous Sovereignty*. Minneapolis, MN: University of Minnesota Press, 2015.

Nakamura, Jeanne, and Mihaly Csikszentmihályi. "Flow Theory and Research." *Handbook of Positive Psychology*, edited by C. R. Snyder et al. Oxford, UK: Oxford University Press, 2001.

Nakata, Sana. "The Infantilisation of Indigenous Australians: A Problem for Democracy." *Griffith Review* 60 (2018) 104–16.

NATSIAC. National Aboriginal and Torres Strait Islander Anglican Council. "Canon 2014." https://anglican.org.au/wp-content/uploads/2019/03/NATSIAC_Canon_2014_updated_GS17.pdf.

———. "Members of NATSIAC at 2016 Gathering Held at Cairns." https://www.natsiac.com/.

NATSICC. National Aboriginal and Torres Strait Islander Catholic Council. "Latest News." http://www.natsicc.org.au/.

NIAA. National Indigenous Australians Agency. "Commonwealth Closing the Gap Annual Report 2022." November 30, 2022. https://www.niaa.gov.au/resource-centre/indigenous-affairs/commonwealth-closing-gap-annual-report-2022.

Niebuhr, H. Richard. *Christ and Culture*. San Francisco: Harper, 2001.

Nungalinya College. "Who Are We?" https://www.nungalinya.edu.au/who-are-we.

Owens, Edward. *The Family Firm: Monarchy, Mass Media, and the British Public 1932–53*. London, UK: University of London Press, 2019.

Pascoe, Bruce. *Dark Emu: Aboriginal Australia and the Birth of Agriculture*. Broome, WA: Magabala, 2018.

Pattel-Gray, Anne. *The Great White Flood: Racism in Australia: Critically Appraised from an Aboriginal Historico-Theological Viewpoint*. Atlanta, GA: Scholars, 1998.

Pike, Elizabeth "Betty." *The Power of Story*. Mulgrave, Victoria: John Garratt, 2010.

Plenary Council. "Reconciliation: Healing Wounds, Receiving Gifts." Fifth Plenary Council of Australia. https://plenarycouncil.catholic.org.au/wp-content/uploads/2022/07/FINAL-Decree-1-Reconciliation-Healing-Wounds-

Rainbow Spirit Elders, *Rainbow Spirit Theology: Towards an Australian Aboriginal theology*. 2nd ed. Hindmarsh, SA: ATF, 2007.

Reconciliation Australia. "What Is National Reconciliation Week?" https://nrw.reconciliation.org.au/about-nrw/.

Regan, Hilary D., and Alan J. Torrance, eds. *Christ and Context: The Confrontation between Gospel and Culture*. London, UK: Bloomsbury, 2016.

Reid, Duncan. *Isn't It Time We Started Listening? Theological Questions Put to Us by Recent Indigenous Writing*. Hindmarsh, SA: ATF, 2020.

Reynolds, Henry. *The Other Side of the Frontier: Aboriginal Resistance to the European Invasion of Australia*. 2nd ed. Ringwood, Victoria: Penguin, 1995.

————. *Why Weren't We Told?: A Personal Search about the Truth of our History*. Ringwood, Victoria: Penguin, 2000.

Ricoeur, Paul. "The Nuptial Metaphor." *Thinking Biblically: Exegetical and Hermeneutical Studies*, edited by André LaCocque and Paul Ricoeur, 265–303. Translated by David Pellauer. Chicago: Chicago University Press, 1998.

Rilke, Rainer Maria. *Letters to a Young Poet*. Translated by Joan M. Burnham. 2nd ed. San Francisco: New World Library, 2000.

Rintoul, Stuart. *The Wailing: A National Black Oral History*. Port Melbourne, Victoria: W. Heinemann, 1993.

Shapiro, Ariel, and Deniz Çam. "Inside the Firm: How the Royal Family's $28 Billion Money Machine Really Works." *Forbes*, March 10, 2021. https://www.forbes.com/sites/arielshapiro/2021/03/10/inside-the-firm-how-the-royal-familys-28-billion-money-machine-really-works/.

Sherwood, John E. "The Moyjil Site, South-West Victoria, Australia: Prologue—of People, Birds, Shell and Fire." *The Royal Society of Victoria* 130 (2018) 7–13.

Steffensen, Victor. *Fire Country: How Indigenous Fire Management Could Help Save Australia*. Richmond, Victoria: Hardie Grant Travel, 2020.

Taylor, Josh. "Indigenous Deaths in Custody Rises to 516 Since the 1991 Royal Commission, Report Says." *The Guardian*, December 20, 2022. https://www.theguardian.com/australia-news/2022/dec/20/indigenous-deaths-in-custody-rises-to-516-since-the-1991-royal-commission-report-says.

Tracy, David. *Blessed Rage for Order: The New Pluralism in Theology*. Chicago: University of Chicago Press, 1996.

Trible, Phyllis. *Texts of Terror: Literary-Feminist Readings of Biblical Narratives*. Minneapolis, MN: Fortress, 2022.

"Uluru Statement from the Heart." https://ulurustatemdev.wpengine.com/wp-content/uploads/2022/01/UluruStatementfromtheHeartPLAINTEXT.pdf.

Ungunmerr, Miriam-Rose. "Dadirri: Inner Deep Listening and Quiet Still Awareness." *EarthSong* 4 (2017) 14–15.

Uniting Church in Australia. *Basis of Union, Constitutions and Regulations 2018 with Covenanting Statement, Code of Ethics and Manual for Meetings*. Sydney, NSW: Uniting Church Assembly, 2018. https://assembly.uca.org.au/images/stories/Regulations/2018/2018_Constitution__Regulations.pdf.

————. "Day of Mourning 2023 #UCADayofMourning." https://uniting.church/dayofmourning/.

————. "The New Preamble." *Uniting Church Studies* 1, no. 16. Sydney, NSW: United Theological College, 2010.

————. "Revised Preamble to the Constitution." Uniting Church in Australia Assembly. https://assembly.uca.org.au/hef/item/668-the-revised-preamble.

University of Divinity. "Vision and Governance." https://divinity.edu.au/university/school-of-indigenous-studies/vision-and-governance/.

Warrior, Robert Allen. "A Native American Perspective: Canaanites, Cowboys and Indians." In *Voices from the Margin: Interpreting the Bible in the Third World*, edited by R. S. Sugirtharajah, 283–90. Maryknoll, NY: Orbis, 2016.

Watego, Chelsea. *Another Day in the Colony*. St. Lucia, QLD: University of Queensland Press, 2021.

Wheeling, Kate. "Australia's Most Extreme Bushfire Season, Statistically Speaking." *Eos* 101 (2020). https://eos.org/research-spotlights/australias-most-extreme-bushfire-season-statistically-speaking.

Wontulp-Bi-Buya College. "Celebrating 40 Years in 2023." https://www.wontulp.qld.edu.au/.

Woodley, Randy S. *Indigenous Theology and the Western Worldview: A Decolonised Approach to Christian Doctrine*. Grand Rapids, MI: Baker Academic, 2022.

Žižek, Slavoj. *On Belief*. London: Routledge, 2001.